LEADERSHIP
Built On
WHY

One Simple Idea That
Will *Revolutionize* the
Leadership Paradigm
and Transform Your Life!

By
Anni Keffer

Copyright © 2017 by Anni Keffer

Printed in the United States of America

Leadership Built on WHY — One Simple Idea That Will Revolutionize the Leadership Paradigm and Transform Your Life! by Anni Keffer

ISBN 13: 978-1-9849525-1-6

ISBN 10: 198495251X

First Edition

2535 Washington Road, Suite 1120
Pittsburgh, PA 15241

1-800-853-6250

www.AnniKeffer.com

What Others Are Saying About Anni Keffer And Her Strategies

"Anni Keffer gives young ladies an opportunity to be able to see what's out there and a direction to go in!"

> — **Joe Theismann,** NFL Legend World Champion and TV Commentator

"Anni ROCKS the stage. She is ABSOLUTELY amazing! Anni will become one of the top female speakers in the world!"

> — **James Malinchak,** featured on ABCs Hit TV Show, *Secret Millionaire*

"Anni Keffer is an expert in leadership and identity. She is a powerful woman with the capacity to lead. She leads the way for all of us!"

> — **Leeza Gibbons,** New York Times Best Selling Author, Emmy Award-Winning TV Host

"Anni is an amazing speaker beyond her years. She connects, inspires and transforms her audience with her content. I recommend Anni!"

> — **Sandra Joseph,** Legendary Broadway Star of *Phantom Of The Opera*, Seen on *Oprah*, *Today* and *The View*

"Anni Keffer is an extraordinary young woman who lives her message and walks her talk! Anni will connect and engage with them on their level and be a positive role model for them. I strongly encourage you to make Anni a part of your next event— you will be so happy you did!"

> — **Julie Carrier,** Emmy Nominated TV Personality, Teen Success Coach

"Our students were very engaged by Anni's enthusiastic speaking style. She kept the students attention the whole time. She did a great job inspiring our students and was very easy for me to work with. I would heartily recommend her."

> — **Bob Montague,** Principal King's Ridge School

"Anni Keffer is a gifted speaker who relates and connects with her audience. Her passion and principles are inspiring and she has a transforming message. I recommend her for your next event."

> — **John Stahl-Wert,** International Best-Selling Author of The Serving Leader, President-Newton Institute

"Anni is energizing, engaging and has a way of relating directly to students. I would definitely recommend Anni."

> — **Chuntel Beach,** Community Network Specialist King's Ridge School

THE IDEAL PROFESSIONAL SPEAKER FOR YOUR NEXT EVENT!

Any organization that wants to develop their people to become "extraordinary," needs to hire Anni for a keynote and/or workshop training!

TO CONTACT OR BOOK ANNI TO SPEAK:

2535 Washington Rd. Suite 1120
Pittsburgh, PA 15241

1-800-853-6250

www.AnniKeffer.com

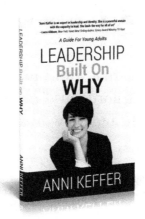

Contents

To my Lord and Savior Jesus Christ,
your love, mercy, constant grace and the cross,
have kept me on this path that you designed for me.
May I honor and glorify you in all that I do.

To my parents, for all you have given,
all you have sacrificed and
how you have loved me, and continue to do so, so beautifully.
I'm continuing to learn and understand what it means
to be a woman of the Lord from you both, and I
wouldn't be here without either of you.

To my brother Josh, your constant love and the example
you set for me has continued to push me to do better,
love better and strive to make a difference
in this world.

To the rest of the ones who have loved,
mentored,
cared,
and championed for me,
I owe the depth of my love and gratitude forever
for helping shape the woman I have become.

WHY YOU NEED THIS BOOK!

WHEN YOU HEAR the word *leadership*, what comes to mind? For most of us, we **think of leadership as the simple concept of**: "The action of leading others."

I don't know about you, but to me, that definition is unclear and misleading.

It's also **incorrect**.

You've been led to believe leadership myths and lies that are **actually** stopping you from being a leader right now, right where you are. What you may not realize is that you have the power to impact your school, your community and your world TODAY—and it's not nearly as difficult as you think.

I wrote this book to show you <u>why</u> that definition of leadership is misleading and also to show you what leadership truly is and what it looks like in your everyday life. We're going to accomplish all of that through a simple examination of two words:

Knowledge + Action

Are you ready? Let's start leading together and impacting our world one day at a time.

Introduction

LEADERSHIP HAS BEEN part of my life since the very beginning.

There was never a time when I wasn't hearing the word "leader"...I can remember—even as a young kid just trying to learn my ABC's—my parents teaching my brother and me about what it means to be a leader.

My dad would say, "Are you a leader or a follower?"

Both of us would respond with, "I'm a leader for God and a follower of Jesus Christ. Blessed by God and destined for greatness."

My brother and I would repeat this phrase every night before bed, at meals, and before school. We were constantly being reminded to be leaders and to aspire and work to accomplish great things.

Even though I didn't fully understand what I was saying in the beginning, repeating this phrase ingrained in me the importance of leadership and greatly influenced the continued impact it would have on me. Then, once I was old enough to better understand what I had been saying all those years, it was already a part of my thoughts, my life and my personal expectations.

Much like your parents expect you to brush your teeth, do your chores, and obey your teachers, leadership became an expectation my parents had for my brother and me. In school, at church, on our sports teams, no matter the circumstance, my parents expected us to step up and lead.

Does that mean we always held leadership positions? No—it meant that no matter what the situation or our assigned role, we were called to lead by example and serve those around us.

My parents did not just *tell* us this; they *modeled* it through their own actions. I saw that my parents were living what they were teaching, which made the concept of leadership really come alive.

Believing the Leadership Lies

It would be easy to think that with such an emphasis placed on leadership in my life, even as a young kid, the rest of my story is predictable. Surely I became a natural born leader and always served as a shining, confident example to others, right?

That is *not* how my story went.

Thanks to the myths and lies about leadership that are ingrained in our society, and that we are being constantly bombarded by, leadership evolved into this idea that became more about following what I *thought* a leader is and is not and what they were "supposed" to do, and less about being a true leader in my everyday life.

I started to believe one of the most known leadership myths, which is that I couldn't lead at a young age. I believed, like you, that I had to wait until I was older to be a leader. I had to bide my time and wait for the day when I was old enough or mature enough or educated enough to be given a leadership title...and more than that, actually be seen as a true leader regardless of my title.

Unfortunately, this belief seeded itself, made deep roots and grew into me choosing not to act. For example, instead of being welcoming to a new kid or going above and beyond expectations in class, I chose to keep to myself and focus inward.

I wasn't stepping up at all; in fact, I was only leading when I was *told* to lead.

Ironic, isn't it?

In my heart, I knew I was destined for greatness and created to do amazing things, but my head was telling me to fit into molds created by other people.

Even though stepping into molds made by other people for me may seem harmless—after all, you are shaped by being taught to fall into certain acceptable standards and molds— it also shaped my behavior through middle school and high school to be totally focused on pleasing other people to the point where I had lost myself completely.

In high school, I found myself believing I was either unable or unqualified to lead as the kind of person I already was and with the knowledge I already had.

Even though I held some leadership positions during that time, I only considered them as such because of some "official title" I was given. Those titles never meant much more than that, and they became roles I played out of a sense of duty to not let the *title* down, rather than out of a desire to impact the people I was expected to lead.

I wasn't looking beyond simple job descriptions to see that there was so much more I was designed to be and to do.

Taking the Power Back

There I was—someone who had been given every opportunity through the right teachings to become a leader—and yet, I was living my life in a mold made by someone else, a mold that didn't fit me or define who I was inside.

At that point, I more or less chose to aimlessly drift about in my life with no real direction or meaning for my future. I deeply struggled to feel that I had purpose or a mission on this Earth.

Have you ever felt that way?

If you can relate to this feeling and to the idea that you are not good enough, smart enough, pretty enough, strong enough, fast enough, just... enough—then I have some great news:

The lies you have been led to believe about your worth and the path you have chosen to follow up until now do NOT have to determine the rest of your life. In fact, the things that have happened to you, the choices you've made in the past, and the things you've experienced will not sculpt your future... unless *you* allow them to.

Your past is not your present, and it is most certainly <u>not</u> your future. The past can be hard and even painful, but it doesn't get to determine the outcome of your life. It has NO power unless you give it power.

The only influence those things should have on your life is to teach you lessons about how to live your life moving forward. They allow you to relate and empathize with more people throughout your life than you could before.

I began to realize that I had the power to change my mindset and my actions to fit who I wanted to become, rather than to fit what the world told me was acceptable for my age, for my gender, and for my particular future.

I *chose* to make the conscious decision to take control and start leading NOW—and you can too.

So many of us struggle to understand why we're even here and what we were created to do. As we go along, trying to find answers, we are told by the media, by our friends, by observation, and sometimes even by those we respect and love most, that we have nothing to offer and are a waste of space; that we are no different from the rest of our peers, and that we should just accept the fact that we are just nameless, faceless numbers.

None of that is true—<u>none</u> of it. Here's the real truth:

You were created for a powerful purpose.

No matter what career path you choose or what business you may start, you are meant to do something powerful with that platform.

Discovering One Life-Changing Word

This sounds so great, doesn't it? Simply choose not to be defined by your past and blaze a new trail. I know you're saying, "Yeah right, Anni. If only you knew my past or what people have said about me."

I know how easy it is to delay that choice and simply stay on the path you "should" be on. Why? Because most of us feel pressure at some point in our lives, pressure to fall in line and do what everyone else is doing. This usually leads to a path that looks something like this (I'm sure this will sound familiar to you, and maybe you are on this path right now):

> *At the beginning of high school, you are told to start thinking about college.*
>
> *Then at 17, you are expected to pick a college and decide on a major and a career before you even know what any of those careers really even mean.*
>
> *In short, you must figure out your <u>entire life</u> before you step into your first college class.*

I remember looking at college after college, but none of them felt right because I didn't even know what I was looking for!

I was faced with what seemed like impossible choices and thought, "How am I supposed to know all of this already? How can I possibly know what I want to do for the rest of my life when I've never lived outside my parents' home?"

So there I was, at a crossroads, feeling that I had no real purpose or mission. I didn't want a cookie cutter life, and I hoped that wasn't really going to be the case. I hoped my purpose was right there, waiting to be unearthed…

And it was.

I finally had *that* moment, one of those rare moments when all the confusion disappears and things finally… click.

I finally saw a glimpse of my purpose, and I just *knew* that there was something more for me than simply taking up space and oxygen on planet Earth.

What I discovered allowed me to begin to realize my gift and passion for teaching and speaking. So I started my own youth leadership speaking company at age 19 and started speaking to middle schools and high schools, youth groups, businesses, and more.

This one breakthrough—this one simple discovery— allowed me, at age 20, to create and host an event for women in Alpharetta, Georgia, and then a year later to become an author and write my very own book.

I still knew I didn't have it all figured out. I knew my purpose would evolve as the years went on. That didn't really matter in the moment. What *really* mattered is that I took action. I wasn't waiting for my perfect purpose or mission to appear in front of me before I did anything.

I paid attention to my passions and my strengths, and I started moving in a direction with the understanding that my path would change and grow as I did.

Did I have everyone on my side, rooting for me? I wish I could say yes, but there were plenty of skeptics and naysayers out there, just waiting to tell me that I wasn't enough and would never make it doing what I was truly passionate about and felt called to do.

But all of the negativity being thrown at me was not powerful enough to overcome what I had begun to discover.

Before I had this breakthrough, I always felt different and out of place compared to my friends, and I didn't like feeling that way—that is, until I became clear about this one thing that changed my perspective. I went from feeling uncomfortable in my own skin to *owning* and even *loving* my individuality—and the power that came with it.

If you feel as though you don't even know where to start concerning your purpose, this one powerful thing will help you too.

It will hand-deliver to you the clarity and focus that you need to begin your journey.

Ready for what it is?

It's your WHY.

Defining, understanding, writing out and pursuing my WHY is what changed my entire life; and it has the power to change yours, as long as you take the time to find out what your WHY is.

Now don't worry, I'm not going to leave you here. We are going to uncover your WHY together.

The rest of this book is devoted to helping you understand what leadership is, discover your WHY, and then take the next purpose-filled steps after this life-changing discovery.

Before we get started, though, allow me to be real with you.

When you desire to be a leader but wake up and feel totally unequipped and unmotivated to pursue this dream... I know what that's like.

When you are viewed as a leader but wonder if you even deserve that perception... I've been there too.

When you feel terrified to show up and lead... I've felt that way as well.

I've walked where you've walked. Yes, our stories may look different, but I've asked the same questions, doubted my abilities and gifts, and wanted to walk away from it all.

Yet through those seasons of self-doubt, I've learned countless lessons that have helped me overcome my fears and insecurities.

This isn't to say that those doubts and insecurities have disappeared completely; they still surface from time to time. But I've learned how to kick them square in the face and put them back in their place—and I can't wait to share with you how to do it!

This book is here to help you walk your leadership path with boldness and bravery while you are impacting everything and everyone around you. So, let's discover your WHY together and then go change the world, one day at a time.

"Leadership is never the title you're given, but the intentional and consistent use of your words and actions."

— *Anni Keffer*

1
Not Your Average Leadership

I DON'T LIKE the word *leadership*.

Surprised to read that? Hear me out.

I'm not fond of the word because it has become a "buzzword," a word or phrase that becomes very popular for a period of time. Buzzwords have become a part of our everyday language, and after a while we say these words without thinking much about their meaning. Examples of widely used buzzwords in the business world include *culture*, *excellence*, *leverage*, *network*, and *synergy*.

Such words are typically used to grab your attention and cause you to think or act in a specific way—and this isn't necessarily a bad thing. The problem is that over time, once a word or phrase is used over and over again, buzzwords lose their original meaning. We say them because we are *supposed* to say them, but they no longer carry the weight or significance they once did.

Those original words once had powerful meanings, and although it's great that so many people are using them, to most of us, they are empty phrases with zero impact.

Leadership has become one of those filler words that I wish would just go away and leave me alone.

Leadership is thrown around in casual conversations, on social media posts, and in school lectures and political speeches. People just *love* to spout off leadership one-liners that make them sound like a walking inspirational quotes book.

The end result? Leadership has become nothing more than an overused cliché.

Time for a Paradigm Shift

Does this mean the word itself has lost all significance? No—but it does mean that we need to become more *intentional* in our use of the word. This is going to require you and me to start paying attention to <u>why</u> we are talking about leadership, and then we must fully realize what we hope to gain by using the word.

Sounds a bit over the top, doesn't it?

Believe me, this is a necessary step—and here's why: Leadership is both an internal *quality* and an external *action*; it's not just "some word" that helps make us sound smarter in conversations.

The real problem with the word is that "leadership" as an idea or action has become far too obscure—its meaning is overly vague and unclear.

It has, in essence, lost all meaning. As a result, people pay about as much attention to it as they do to words such as *and* or *the*.

If someone were to stop you on the street right now and ask you what a "leader" is, what would you even say? If you took a poll of the next 100 people you see, I bet only a handful of them would be able to give you a meaningful definition of the word "leadership."

And yet we _all_ use it _all_ the time!

That's just how we humans seem to operate—we are quick to use buzzwords without really understanding why because we know that they're trending and people will notice them... momentarily. *But it always comes back to the fact that they don't truly understand what the word means at its core.*

That is why I'm proposing a leadership meaning overhaul. When we talk about "leadership" and about "becoming leaders," our goal should be to help other people understand and ultimately change their actions to reflect those of a true leader.

So, from this moment on, you and I must take a stand to use the word leadership, not as a way to help us momentarily look more educated than the next person, but as a real *change catalyst* for our world.

All Talk, No Movement

Of course, this is easier said than done, right? This is partly because in most cases, people are really not paying attention to what you say. I know that sounds harsh, but think about this for a second:

When you meet someone new, aren't you usually thinking things like, "Do I sound smart or interesting?" "What can I say to impress this person?" "Am I talking too much or not enough?" "Do I have something in my teeth?"

The list could go on and on of the internal questions, doubts, and insecurities swirling inside our heads at any given time, couldn't it? Well guess what? If you are thinking those things, so are the people with whom you are talking.

In fact, we are carrying on such a lively conversation inside our own heads that we only hear a small portion of what is being said to us!

The bottom line is that since a lot of what we say isn't ever really even heard, most of us have only a narrow window of opportunity in which to truly influence people with our words. That is why we need to take what we *do* say—in those rare moments when people are paying attention to us—very seriously.

It's been said that you have three seconds with someone to get another 30 seconds, and if you're lucky, maybe another three minutes. In short, the amount of time during which people *really* hear you is fleeting and precious.

Are you using that time wisely?

When you take the time to sound a little different—by explaining a buzzword like leadership, for example, in a unique way—*that* is when intentional, ongoing conversations have the ability to make a big impact on your world. (And don't worry— in the next chapter, I'll give you a great example of how to sound different that you can use right away).

Our culture has diminished the value of meaningful conversations partly because of the fact that meaningful conversations don't really exist anymore. Most of our casual exchanges are pretty much composed of nothing BUT filler words. We say things like; "How are you today?," "How about this weather?," and "What do you like to do?" almost on autopilot.

And now, thanks to the overuse of what was once a powerful term, commands such as, "Step up and be a leader" seem more like what your parents and teachers want you to do rather than what you feel called to do.

We live in a society that knows how to talk; rehearsing what to say, when to say it, and which are the perfect words for the moment. We've become so used to being able to type and retype what we want to say until it's perfect that we've lost the ability to speak in the moment.

We talk and talk without really saying anything at all. Ultimately, the fancy buzzwords and surface responses serve as a mask to cover up how little we know about what we are talking about. We don't want to be seen as fools when we talk, especially to those closest to us, but we aren't willing to ask the questions to truly *understand* our subject matter.

Our world is tired of the clichés. We're ready for something to change. Your words are useless unless they are combined with action.

That is what real leadership is—intentionally and consistently speaking calls to action! Leadership requires understanding... and then movement! You aren't truly leading until you are speaking the words while moving your feet.

You have to be willing to walk the path first, and often times *alone*, before you can expect people to start walking behind you and eventually with you.

We should be leading, being *remarkable* and *innovative*, telling our *stories*, *standing* out and making an *impact*. Unfortunately, these words are going to remain in the category of overused filler words until ***you*** do more with them. They are begging you to take them out for a spin and see how they can transform your life.

What we often forget is what things like telling your story, making an impact, and being remarkable actually do—when you use them properly in your life rather than just talk for the sake of talking—is transform, impact and influence your world. They are meant to shake things up and change the status quo.

> "Successful people do what unsuccessful people are not willing to do."
>
> —*Jim Rohn*

These phrases don't want to be stuck on the sidelines, watching you live your life; they want to be on the field with you, helping you to live out the call for your life. You can live out these calls to action in your school, sports team, job, and really, anywhere.

The people today who make the biggest difference in our world are those who willingly speak about change, and most importantly, live out that change. Because, when you think about it, change speaks and acts for itself. And believe me, people notice when someone is willing to say and do the things other people aren't.

Shatter the Status Quo

You can't lead, be remarkable, or tell your story, in any capacity, until you understand what true leadership really looks like and how to continually live it out every day.

This book will turn your view of leadership on its head, and that's where it should stay. Real leadership isn't what you are being *told* it is, and it certainly doesn't look like most people's interpretation of it as a modern buzzword.

Up until now, the cookie cutter form of leadership has involved doing things the way they've always been done; it's been easy, simple and average. No one questions you, looks at you strangely, or thinks you're crazy.

When you do what everyone else in your class is expected to do and when you do and say exactly what everyone else at work does and says, then guess what? You'll look, feel, and act like every other person on the planet, and that's where they want you to stay—in the nice, neat little box they have built for you.

The rest of society will have already labeled you, put you where you belong, and feel comfortable knowing that everyone is in his or her place as just another faceless number.

Is that how the world gets changed? Is that how to revolutionize your life? No—and for those of us who are called and feel led to do more, do you know what you have to do? Rip right out of that box, hand it back to society, say "Thank you, but no thank you," and then lead, impact and influence like never before!

Those who are willing to dream wild and crazy dreams, follow those dreams through action, and ultimately kill the status quo, are those who have successfully broken out of their neat, comfortable boxes.

We are talking about real leaders such as Martin Luther King Jr., Mother

"Even if you've had a negative effect on others in the past, you can turn that around and make your impact a positive one."
—*John C. Maxwell*

Teresa, Henry Ford, Abraham Lincoln, Blake Mycoskie, and Ashley LeMieux. We are talking about the movers and shakers who challenge what's expected and who question the status quo because the status quo is broken and certainly not making our world any better.

In fact, the willingness to keep following the status quo is making our world worse. Our system of constantly doing everything the same has led us to lead average lives, with average impact and average results.

You will always have choices in your life, hundreds of choices (some big and some small) to make literally every day. What time will you choose to wake up in the morning? Which spaghetti sauce should you choose? What movie do you want to watch? Should you get whipped cream on your mochaccino?

And that's just the beginning. That's just the simple stuff. Now, here are some other not-so-simple choices:

- Do I want to be average or the best?

- Do I choose to be mediocre or outstanding?

- Do I want to influence others or submit to conformity?

- Will I have an impact or abide by the status quo?

What will you choose, and who will you challenge yourself to be? Are you willing to step out of a comfortable, average life and into a powerful, outstanding call that will change you and those around you?

This is your starting point. Regardless of past and present, mistakes, failures, and regrets, start new. Lead now. Look around for new and fresh ways to reignite your passion for change.

Surprising Sources of Inspiration

For some of you, this may be the first time you are hearing these ideas. You may have even thought living this kind of life was never possible.

I'm telling you it is—and I'm giving you permission to boldly blaze a new path, to reach for something you think is way too big, too scary or too daring.

This is your time.

This is your opportunity to throw mediocrity and the status quo out the door and out of your life.

Despite what the world says, what the media shows or what the naysayers whine about, YOU can lead and change your world. All of those people are really just there to remind you to keep your eyes focused on your WHY, on your journey, and on those following and supporting you.

Many (if not most) people will call you an impractical dreamer; they'll tell you that what you're doing sounds "nice" but is just unrealistic; they'll tell you that you'll just end up disappointed; others will tell you that you're too young; some will even tell you to stop what you're doing.

Respond with kindness, love and respect to these naysayers, but don't listen to them. In fact, here is the best thing to do with the critics, bullies and naysayers:

Thank them.

Yep, you read that right.

Thank the people who said you couldn't, those who said you were too young or too stupid, the people who said you were just a dreamer with your head in the clouds.

Every time they say something, write something, or whisper something mean, negative or just plain rude, I literally want you to say, "Thank you."

> "If you are not creating a negative response from somebody, you're not fascinating to anybody."
>
> —**Sally Hogshead**

You are not going to say it with sarcasm—because you really should mean it! Thank them for the negative comments because you'll look back one day and realize those remarks spurred you on to greater things, just as it has done for other world changers throughout history.

In fact, if all the past and present great leaders of the world listened to such people, our world would not have seen the change or accomplishments we have seen over these past 238 years.

Whether you choose to do this to their face, in your head, or in an online response, gracefully and kindly say thank you for the negative words, doubt, and cynicism.

You don't need anyone's permission to be a leader. You are one NOW! And you certainly don't need a stamp of approval—which is good, because you won't get one.

Be YOU and let them be them. At the end of each day, you can lay your head on your pillow knowing you were boldly YOU, feeling proud that you loved your haters, and celebrating the fact that you impacted and influenced your world.

Then move forward and go kick some leadership butt.

You (Yes, You!) ARE Ready For This

Now that you've been given this charge to go "be a leader," I don't want you to feel overwhelmed, nor do I want you to think you now have to live up to some lofty standard of leadership. Leadership doesn't mean you have to start your own business, found a nonprofit, become a speaker, or get into politics. You can be a leader as a nurse, a teacher, a CEO, a student, a musician, an athlete, a mom or dad, a plumber, a construction worker, and everything in between.

The dream itself doesn't matter because everyone is different and unique. What matters is this: whatever you choose to do, you decide to lead in that role and always have a strong, passionate WHY that compels you to move forward and take action, whatever that action may look like for your life.

We are going to spend the last half of the book talking about this WHY and how you can hone in on it, but before we go there, you need to understand and then commit to these new and uncommon ideas about what it really means to lead right now, in the life you are living today.

Most people don't believe they can lead at a young age. Just like I did, they believe they have to be in college or be an adult with a "real" job or have a title that someone gave to them. Real talk? These can be the *worst* kind of leaders. You know why? Because leaders just by title only aren't motivated or inspired beyond the simple, "I'm supposed to be a leader, so let me do what's expected of me."

Other people believe that they can never be leaders because of their personality, their communication style, past or present mistakes or experiences, or the fact that they don't feel accepted or loved.

Here is where those myths and lies stop: RIGHT HERE.

You—with your gifts, talents, flaws and mistakes, with your experiences, your hurt, your triumphs and your dreams—you can be a leader.

It is **your** choice, no one else's. No one gets to choose your destiny for you.

Everything you bring to the table—both the good and bad—helps you to be an even better leader if you let it. Not everyone will agree with that or with your decision to lead, but guess what? Who cares?

Now is the time to stop allowing other people to dictate your decisions and your direction. This is your life, your impact and your influence. Will you squash your potential by following others simply because it's easier than standing up for what you want? Or will you choose to walk out into what God has created you to be and to do?

This is your time; start young!

Leaders create and support movements that implement long-term change and impact. You don't do what you do simply because it's your job or what you believe you should be doing. Pure leadership goes beyond the average, the everyday, and the normal.

It's about something bigger than you—but that doesn't mean it has to be some global movement. It starts with where you are, who you are and where you want to go, and then finding people who connect with that idea.

Those people? Author and entrepreneur Seth Godin calls them your "tribe." These will be the people who will help you start your movement. They may be few and far between, but as you start to share your WHY and break out of your box, you will start to add people to your tribe, and together, you and your tribe can swim upstream and change the status quo.

Don't wait until you are the "right age." You were made to do great things NOW. Start leading, influencing and making mistakes, failing and picking yourself back up to keep walking the path.

This is your time to lead...you have the power to change the world for good

> "The visionary starts with a clean sheet of paper, and re-imagines the world."
> *—Malcolm Gladwell*

or for bad, or you can leave this world the same, as though you never even existed. Choose now what you wish to do with the time you have been given on this Earth.

Let's walk together on this journey of discovering what true leadership is, finding your WHY, and choosing your level of influence and impact. As we continue on this path to discovering your WHY, the next stop includes two words that will change your life. Are you ready? Turn the page...

"Your biggest frustrations with the world often stem from what you are most passionate about and what you will be most likely to change."

-Anni Keffer

2

"I Believe"

I MAY NOT know you personally, but I have a feeling you've been asked these questions before:

"Have you picked a major yet?"

"What are your career plans after college?"

I've heard them both A LOT—and truthfully, I can't stand them.

I know people are trying to be polite; they are just conversation starters, right? At least they are *supposed* to be. Unfortunately, as soon as we start in with the "normal" and expected (aka boring) response, we lose our audience. Here is the Normal Response:

I am majoring in (blank).

I am a (blank).

I am going to do (blank).

Imagine this with me: You run to the store for toothpaste, deodorant and Sun Chips. You quickly try to find the shortest line, hoping your line-picking skills landed you in the fast lane. You pick a line and commit to it, but only then do you lay your eyes upon the most horrifying sight.

The woman three shoppers ahead of you has a mountain of items in her cart and it appears—as she brings out a large folder overflowing with clippings—that she is attempting to pay for all 70 of her items with coupons.

By the time she is finally done checking out, you've paged through every single tabloid—twice. You've called all of your friends, your mom, and your grandma. You also polished off the bag of Sun Chips and are ready for another one.

With two more people still in front of you, you decide to strike up a conversation with the man directly ahead of you, a man you soon find out is named John. You and John make some small talk and before you know it, he asks you the inevitable question:

"So, what do you do?"

You are ready with the normal, expected answer; as a result, John zones out after a few seconds, the conversation dwindles, and you go on to ask the same question and John responds just the same.

That's a pretty typical exchange, right? Happens every day across the country. It's probably happening somewhere right now.

With that kind of a conversation, there is no connection. There was no value in what you said; it was normal, ordinary, and highly forgettable. You've given the same rehearsed answer that everyone else gives.

It's not about what you believe. Instead, it's about giving the boring, expected (and therefore socially acceptable) response to a common question.

Why do we all do this? The simple answer is because saying the expected response is comfortable; it virtually guarantees that no one will look at you as though you just sprouted a second nose, and you'll be able to slide by without being noticed for the work you're doing or the words you are speaking.

Everybody does it—and yet, what you just created was really a lost opportunity. You've taken away John's opportunity to hear your story, to stand behind something that may resonate with him, or to be inspired by what YOU BELIEVE.

Maybe your "I believe" is exactly what John would have needed to hear in order to keep going, to chase after his own "I believe," or do something with his day that he figured no one would notice if he did or didn't do.

This isn't about your "I believe" being so mind blowing that everyone will stand in awe of what you say. Sharing your "I believe" statement is about connecting with people, telling your story and revealing part of the real you to others.

Why is that important? Because the simple act of being courageous enough to tell your "I believe" can change the world. Sure, that's a lofty goal, but then again, the best goals generally are.

All it takes is that first step, that first time, of stepping out and standing up to have an important—and maybe even a little uncomfortable—conversation that can lead to real change.

A Fresh Response to a Tired Question

Of course, it's not the statement itself that changes the world; it's the action that follows the "I believe" that matters. Think about some of the brands that have made headlines by telling the world what they believe, and then going out there, taking action, and making a difference:

- **TOMS**. This amazing shoe company founded by Blake Mycoski features the "One for One" program, which promises that for every single product purchased, TOMS will give a pair of shoes to someone in need.

- **Sevenly**. The clothing brand was founded in 2011 with the mission of leading a generation toward generosity. They create what they call "7-day cause campaigns," inviting customers to purchase products that donate to nonprofits.

- **Warby Parker.** The eyewear makers believe that everyone has the right to see. So Warby Parker partners with non-profits like VisionSpring to ensure that for every pair of glasses sold, a pair is distributed to someone who desperately needs one.

These brands aren't just *telling* us what they believe; they're going out and *doing* what they believe. They are bringing together the most powerful combination needed for change to happen:

WORDS + ACTION

Do you know WHY you exist on this planet? The people around you want to know—I promise! Do you want people to know the real you? They can! In fact, people are desperate to hear anything other than the expected responses.

Despite what we've been led to believe, people aren't interested in your <u>ordinary facade</u>, but rather your <u>extraordinary heart</u>.

So, what if *you* changed the conversation? What if you led from your heart rather than deliver the response everyone is expecting to hear?

To see what this might look like, let's shake up that exchange with John from earlier. What if, instead of giving the expected answer, you began with the brave response:

"I believe..."

And when John asks, "So, what do you do?" your answer sounds something like this:

*Well John, **I believe** that each and every person was created with a unique mission and purpose. **I believe** we were all created to do something extraordinary with our lives, whether that happens in our families, our communities or the world. But I didn't always believe I was created for a purpose. I struggled to believe I was worth anything or had anything of value to offer.*

After working through that, I knew I didn't want other kids to struggle as I had. So a few years ago I started to speak in high schools and middle schools sharing this exact message. I then expanded my message into a mentoring program as well as an event called "Young Women of Influence," which is a day and a half where girls come together to learn more about their purpose and mission, as well as what real leadership looks like.

What do you think John might do? I'll tell you—John might just fall over.

Most people don't have the courage to speak in such a manner! It would completely turn the conversation upside down, and your impact and reach would skyrocket.

What if John had a sister who was struggling with her belief about who she is and what she was made to do? Within 15 seconds, you just informed him of the existence of a resource that could help his sister become more grounded in her mission and purpose.

What this type of response displays is real leadership—and this kind of leadership always comes back to the idea that this life isn't really about you. Making a difference and stepping up to lead in a world full of followers isn't about how to make YOU feel better or more worthy or smarter.

Lead with your "I believe" because *that* is what people connect and resonate with. That's what even the most casual of acquaintances, such as the guy in front of you at the store connects with and wants to hear more about.

The Johns and Janes of the world want to know **why** I started speaking, not just that "I speak."

When you just talk about what you do, you sound like everyone else. ***People aren't asking for your job description; they want to hear your mission statement.*** People want to get behind a mission, a cause, and a purpose. They are looking for those whose purpose is to make an impact and leave the world better than they found it.

After one of my recent speeches, one of the audience members approached me and asked whether it was hard to have those "I believe" conversations and what kind of response I got when I did have them.

My candid and honest answer was this: "When I first started having these conversations, it was incredibly uncomfortable and unnatural. A lot of times I shied away from having them simply because I was afraid. Yet every time I led with my "I believe," I never once regretted it."

So yes, it will be weird and awkward when you start trying to lead with your "I believe." But anything worth doing is never easy. If it scares you, then you're on the right path.

All too often, we interpret feelings of fear, discomfort, and awkwardness as signs that we must not be saying the right things and we should probably just stop. Just like a child learning to read, you have to fight past those times when you "aren't saying it right," because eventually you will!

All of what you are feeling is natural and normal (being uncomfortable equals progress), so never use those feelings as excuses to stop being intentional with your words.

Two Words, Endless Possibilities

People want to join a revolution. And if you think you are "too [blank]" or "not [blank] enough" to be a part of something revolutionary, then it's time to start thinking bigger.

Whether you're starting a clothing line, writing an album or working on cars, if you tell and then *show* people your mission, the right people will rise up behind you.

When combined, "I" and "believe" are two of the most powerful words in the English language; they are powerful enough to change your community, your school and your world; they are mighty enough to start movements that can change the course of history.

It might be hard for you to consider that just two simple words can accomplish so much. All I say to that is that it's a good thing Martin Luther King Jr. didn't think so. King's movement was based on what he believed; he shared those beliefs and those dreams with the world, and as a result, he changed our world as we know it.

His "I believe" was that he had a dream and he lived out that dream through his words and actions both publicly and privately. As he started to share this, people began to gather behind him, and they started to lead with their own "I believe" statements—and with that, they changed the world.

Mother Teresa led with what she believed and not only touched countless thousands of lives, but also revolutionized what it meant to serve and touch people simply by meeting them where they are, with all their faults and flaws.

We so often limit ourselves by thinking that the scope of what we can actually change is insignificant at best. We are just one little person, after all. This is yet another myth that has been spread as truth for years. **The reality is that even the smallest changes can snowball into bigger and greater changes.**

Something as simple as having conversations that start with "I believe" has the power to make incredible changes as long as you are intentional, sincere, and continue having those conversations at every opportunity.

> "The secret of leadership is simple: Do what you believe in. Paint a picture of the future. Go there. People will follow."
>
> —*Seth Godin*

Are you willing to be brave enough to have "I believe" conversations?

_____

_____

Would you be okay if you were the only one having those conversations for a while?

_____

_____

If you answered yes to both questions, then get ready to see lives affected around you. Change doesn't start when everyone is on board. Change starts when one person is willing to step out alone and do something directly in line with their WHY that people can resonate with on a deeper level.

We all believe something, and it's time to let the world know by starting "I believe" conversations every chance you get!

Throughout this book, you are going to learn a lot about things like purpose, mission, and of course, your WHY. Just remember that these two little words—I BELIEVE—are absolutely the simplest and most effective way to start a conversation that can change the world.

"You can't tell people to start walking a mile of a journey you haven't already been walking for two miles."

—*Anni Keffer*

3

BE the Change

"BE THE CHANGE you wish to see in the world."

That's a famous quote by Mahatma Gandhi. Have you ever wondered what that even means?

I couldn't figure it out for years. After hearing it over and over again, it just sounded like a nice motivational quote that teachers like to use to sound philosophical or speakers might recite to motivate their audiences.

How many times have you heard this quote? Personally, I've lost count. It's clichéd on the regular, tattooed too much, and spoken too nonchalantly.

Truthfully, I was sick of hearing it. Yes, I liked it, but because I didn't understand its true meaning, it had no real value to me. So I stopped paying attention to it altogether. That is, until I was in the exact right place to finally hear it for what it was actually saying.

This exact right place was at the foot of a Mt. Everest-sized problem in my life. I knew this mountain had to be moved, but I didn't know how to move it.

An impossible feat, right? It simply can't be done; no one person can move a mountain on their own.

At least that's what it seemed that everyone was telling me; that there was nothing that a 17-year-old girl from Pittsburgh could do about this Mt. Everest problem.

Want to know what this problem was? I'll tell you—I was sick and tired of being bombarded with the constant media messages that tell you and me:

You aren't good enough, pretty enough,
smart enough, or cool enough.

You aren't enough...

Unless you do, say and act a certain way.

Unless you have these clothes, this phone or this car.

If you live the way the rest of us live—status quo obsessed,
inside your little box, and focused totally inward—you will
be enough.

Doing, saying, looking, acting, thinking, or wearing anything
outside of what we decide is acceptable makes you not enough.

I have no doubt that you have felt this pressure at some point in your life. It's almost impossible not to. From the time we are barely old enough to understand what pressure even is, the *pressure* to conform and to fit in with a set of acceptable standards set by some unknown and judgmental "all-seeing eye" begins.

We buy into these lies and start believing them as truths. Even though I recognized these lies for what they were, I was still struggling not to believe these things myself.

All this false and deceptive message is really succeeding in accomplishing is making people buy certain products, go to the "right" school, look a particular cookie-cutter way, and most devastatingly, never believe they could do the very things they were created to do.

Same Quote, New Perspective

I knew this message (lie) had to change—but I had absolutely no idea how I was going to change it.

At first, I tried complaining about it...constantly. Didn't help. Then I moved to the *highly* effective technique of yelling at my TV and my phone. Not surprisingly, those tactics changed nothing.

I was left with some well-timed eye rolling and overall feelings of annoyance, frustration, and helplessness.

Do you know why I was frustrated? It's because I am so deeply passionate about you, your generation and those who will come after you. My desire is for you to understand that you have an amazing, unbelievable mission and a purpose for which you were uniquely created.

I *want* and *need* you to know that you can influence those around you in a positive, life-changing way—if you choose to do so.

Watching my generation and the younger generations believe absolute garbage about who we are and who we are created to be—well, it made me pretty freaking livid. Add to that the fact that I *felt* like there was nothing I could do to change anything, and it made everything so much worse.

But then, something magical happened.

Remember that Gandhi quote we've all heard way too many times?

"Be the change you wish to see in the world."

I finally got it—and it didn't matter anymore that is was too clichéd, overly tattooed, and said too nonchalantly. It finally clicked, and this time, it changed my entire perspective.

BE.

It's the word I had been missing the whole time! I had read that quote over and over again and yet had somehow glossed over that first word every single one of those times!

Gandhi wasn't telling us to go sit on a ledge somewhere and dream of change.

Gandhi wasn't telling us that talking about the change is what matters or makes any sort of difference.

He said to **BE**. If you want change, you first have to **BE** the change.

Gandhi was telling us to stop wishing or hoping things will change and just become the kind of change you wish the world would embrace!

Model it. Act it out. Be a doer. Take action.

Instead of just flapping your lips, start moving your feet.

You don't like something? Well, fix it or shut up about it! If all you do is complain about something changing or not changing, no one will follow you. Nothing was changing about my Mt. Everest problem because I wasn't willing to do anything to change it.

If you want people to follow, start moving! Walk the path first. Then look for people to get behind you. If you aren't willing to walk first, then others won't be willing to begin the walk at all.

The Journey of a Lifetime

In 2006, Blake Mycoskie needed a vacation. At age 30, he was working on his fourth business in seven years and decided to travel to Argentina for a break. He loved Argentina; he loved the culture, the people and even the *alpargata*, which is a canvas shoe that everyone in the country was wearing at the time.

One day, he met an American woman heading up a shoe drive for the millions of people in Argentina without anything to wear on their feet. Not having shoes affects the Argentinians' ability to get food and water for their families. It's especially hard on children; it makes it more difficult for them to get to school, and constantly walking around barefoot also causes them to be more susceptible to various diseases.

Blake couldn't shake the sight of people living without shoes in village after village, but how could he possibly get all of these children the shoes they needed? He was staring at his Mt. Everest problem—millions of kids without shoes and no clear or easy way to provide those shoes to them.

Blake had a choice:

He could choose to complain, be frustrated, sit at home and worry about those precious kids without shoes.

Or.

He could BE the change he wished to see in Argentina, and in the rest of the world.

Blake courageously started TOMS, which operates according to the "One for One" business model, where for every shoe purchased, a child in need receives a pair of shoes. Since 2006, TOMS has provided over 50 million shoes to children to need—and the number is only growing.

This kind of leadership—to first **BE** the change—is about stepping up before anyone else does. It's about stepping out into uncharted territory when no one else is willing. It's also about accepting the fact that you may be the only one out there for while, because most people aren't willing to take the first step before someone else does it first.

When you have a Mt. Everest problem that speaks to your WHY and you're ready to see a change, it starts with you stepping out ahead—and that's the scariest part. The first step, peeking your head out to see that to your left and to your right there is no one but you. There may be people ahead, but often they seem too far away to feel like they're walking with you.

The simple act of stepping out on the path of your mission will cause people to pay attention. Then, as you pair that with having conversations about your Mt. Everest problem and how you are **BE**ing the change, people will want to get on board with what you're doing.

The journey toward solving your own Mt. Everest problem could be a short one—or it could take a lifetime. The kind of leadership and thinking I'm proposing in this book takes looking at life on a long-term scale, meaning you aren't concerned that things haven't drastically changed in a week, month or even a year.

Looking at life on a grander scale will allow you not to be worried about short-term mistakes, failures and setbacks. Instead, you can stay dedicated to always being the kind of leader that focuses on stepping out in front, staying obsessed over your WHY, and moving towards building others up through positive and lasting change.

As a bonus, the people around you who have a short-term, instant gratification view of life—those who like to tell you that your mission needs to be done differently or not at all—can be more easily ignored.

As a way to keep you going and fueled for your journey, you'll no doubt experience some short-term wins along the way. You'll likely also find that things start to change more quickly or more slowly than you expected; you just keep your focus on where you're going and let the speed of the journey adjust to where it needs to be.

Speaking of focus, where is yours? For me, my Mt. Everest problem was the catalyst that uncovered my WHY. Maybe you have yet to recognize your own Mt. Everest problem, so I'd like to take a moment and ask you to answer some questions that I guarantee no one has ever asked you before.

These questions are going to go a long way toward helping you define your purpose and mission in life (which are both part of your WHY... you'll learn all about those in the next few chapters).

My hope is that these unconventional questions will get you thinking about how to hone in on the Mt. Everest problem in this world that compels you to DO and to BE.

1. What dream did you trade in or what dream are you considering trading in to feel accepted or loved?

_____

_____

_____

_____

_____

2. Knowing that you are going to fail at first, what new thing will you try?

_____

_____

_____

_____

_____

3. If you could fix one problem in the world, what would it be and why?

_____

_____

_____

_____

_____

_____

What most people don't understand is that passion is the RESULT of action, not the CAUSE of it. So just starting ACTING and BEing today, and your passion will overflow as a result!

Fight Your Instincts

Your life was not meant to be average, and that means that average, vanilla leadership just won't do. You need to display the kind of leadership that can turn a community, a state, and a whole nation upside down and inside out. It's not rocket science—it's accomplished by serving those in your purpose and passion and helping them get to where they need to go.

The journey may be a thousand miles, but you can BE today. Right now. You simply start by changing the conversation.

You do what you do because of what you believe not just because it's your job. This is called ***servant leadership***— and servant leadership calls for your journey to be lead by a belief and a calling rather than by what you *think* you need to be doing.

Another part of practicing servant leadership is to understand that we ***all*** have Mt. Everest problems we so desperately long to change. Only, nothing happens until you first <u>*become*</u> the change you are looking for in this world. You can share that with the world and empower others to move their own mountains.

Too often I see people who truly want to affect change but then turn around to the people they want to help and treat them in the same way they were treated. Martin Luther King, Jr. did not allow this to happen. When he was treated with violent contempt, he called for love and peace. He was **BE**ing the change; he wanted African Americans to be treated as equals, so he treated the very people hurting him and his people with love and peace and as equals.

This takes a supernatural strength—and one that does not come naturally. In fact, our instinct often works against us in such instances. When a Mt. Everest problem surfaces and negatively impacts part of who we are, our instinct is to lash out and to fight for justice.

But if the change you're longing for is that people would not act that way, why are *you* acting that way?

This is hard, but if you can do it—if you can fight nature and treat others according to the Golden Rule rather than according to the way you may have been treated up to now—you'll reap lasting, enormous rewards. This requires the discipline to stay true to what you believe and what you long to change.

You also have to be secure in knowing those other people may never change. Even with you treating them correctly, they may still choose to act the same way. You'll never be able to control *their* actions or words—you can only control *your* actions, decisions and mindset.

Too often, we become obsessed with trying to fix other people and control how they act towards others. Well, stop trying, because if you think you can fix anyone, you're chasing an impossible dream.

Now, you may have resonated with everything we've talked about up until this point, and now you're wondering, "Okay, so what's my **WHY**? How do I even figure it out?"

Let's talk about this simple, three-letter word and discover exactly why it means *everything* in your journey.

"Part of your purpose here on Earth is to give others the space and freedom to breath a sigh of relief and say, 'I'm so glad I'm not alone.'"

—*Anni Keffer*

4

What is 'WHY' Anyway?

BY NOW, YOU have gained a much better understanding of two things: 1) You know why the word "leadership" as a buzzword is useless, and 2) You also know what *real* servant-based leadership looks and feels like, the kind that moves mountains and changes the world when it is born out of your "I believe" statement.

That was the first step in your pre-journey as you collect the knowledge you need that will empower you to take that first step into the journey you were *born* to take.

Now comes part two, and that is defining and understanding your WHY.

Without your own personal defined WHY, any form of leadership you undertake is essentially a waste. Your WHY is also what steers you away from selfishly leading for *you* and what *you* want, which is a form of leadership that will either fail instantaneously or not too far down the line.

Leadership without a WHY becomes about you, and will ultimately not work to change the status quo.

Without your WHY steering the ship, we look to fill our lives with all of the things we're told we need to have in order to be enough; we search for ways to fill the emptiness because our existence alone never feels like it's enough.

A self-fulfilling form a leadership won't be enough on good days, and it will break you down even more on bad days—and for this reason the WHY is the most critical, influential and sustaining part of your leadership.

Think of it this way: Could a plumber, electrician, and roofer come do their part in the building of a new home without having the foundation in place first? They could try, but it would never stand.

No one would ever skip laying the foundation when building a house, so why do we do it in our lives? Your WHY is the complete foundation, and if you don't build it properly, or at all, you can't begin to lead and impact others.

That foundation—your WHY—will change the entire game.

Countdown to Launch

Ever look at amazing artists, athletes, and company founders and wonder how they create so much and do what they do every day?

They *must* have more hours in a day than we do, right?

As much as it might help your ego to think that Beyonce can do what she does only because she has the money to hire assistants and other people to do the things she doesn't want to do, the bottom line is that the superstars and business moguls of the world got to where they are today using the same 24 hours a day to which we all have access.

Of course, this still begs the question: How in the world are they able to create and do amazing things that impact so many people?

All of those people that you look up to and see getting so much done are where they are because of how intentionally they spend their time, money and what they think about. They've also learned to say no (a lot), and they are crystal clear about where they are and where they are headed.

It all comes back to finding your WHY, which is the foundation for what you are doing, who you are doing it for, and how you do it. Once that is determined, you spend less time trying to figure out what you're doing with your life and you...

Just. Do. It.

Here is why that is vitally important: We spend so many years of our lives thinking about how we're going to spend the rest of our lives that we miss all of the time we could be living and making an impact!

Once NASA prepares to launch a rocket by determining its mission and figuring out *why* they are spending millions of dollars to send it into the great beyond, they don't wait around to send it off into space. It doesn't sit on the launch pad for the next two years. It has its coordinates set and it takes off to go make things happen!

Your WHY gives you your coordinates—and those coordinates provide you with the ability to stay the course when things get tough, the road becomes too rough, the world doesn't make sense, and you fail and make mistakes.

Your WHY is your greater sense of purpose; it gives your life the definition it needs so that you don't become defined by your career, your passions, or your interests. For example, if you love to play sports, you aren't just an athlete; you play your sport for a greater reason than just for the fun of the game.

You aren't just a musician; you play and write music for a greater purpose.

You aren't just a student; you learn and grow because you are building a future for yourself in which you plan to accomplish great things.

Most of your friends and peers aren't thinking like this. They aren't looking to be leaders and impact others now or down the road—and this won't be their mindset in high school, college and beyond. The majority of my friends in high school and college weren't thinking about this either.

So what does that mean for you? It means that they either won't understand what you're doing, won't like it, or will only cheer you on from a distance.

I know—that doesn't sound too exciting. Well, here's the deal: you aren't defining your WHY to be liked, popular or voted "most likely to succeed" in your graduating class. You're doing this because you were made to have influence and impact. You were created to change the world and leave it better than you found it.

Let's look at this on a deeper level:

WHY:
The reason you believe you were put on this Earth.
What you were created to do.

An important note: Your purpose, passion and mission aren't fixed. They will change and evolve, just as you do. Your journey of discovering these is just that, a *journey*. The point of discovering all of these isn't to look for a single destination, but rather to be intentional with the journey and make the most of every season you find yourself in.

For instance, my WHY is to impact the next generation and to teach them about leadership, their identity and value. The way I go about doing that can be done in so many various forms. I'm the one responsible for living out my WHY no matter what season I find myself in, what job I have or what's going on in the world.

You might not think a job in retail, fast food or sales is part of your WHY and your purpose, and yet it is. I had a retail job in which I could live out my WHY in every time I showed up for work. If I had chosen not to live out my WHY in that particular season of my life while I held that position, it would have been on *me*, not on the job.

So let's get right down to it...

What is your WHY?

_____

_____

_____

_____

_____

_____

_____

_____

_____

_____

_____

_____

_____

_____

_____

_____

**Tear this page out
and hang it up!**

The Most Pointless Pursuit

Was writing down your WHY difficult for you? Or was that WHY already burning a hole through your pen, just waiting to get onto the paper?

Either way, congratulations for taking the step of writing it down in the first place!

And now, let's address that elephant in the room. This elephant will always come stomping in when you try something new, do something differently or attempt to grow in any new or uncomfortable way.

The elephant in the room is *Perfection*.

Most of us wrestle with the idea of perfection—pursuing it, attaining it, and defining it in our lives. Perfection always seems to know the worst possible times to rear its ugly head, and one of those times will almost assuredly be in the pursuit of your WHY, especially in the beginning of your journey.

Since this is inevitable, I need to tell you a big secret to success:

Your WHY will never be perfect.
And you shouldn't try to make it perfect.

Life is messy, and at times, it's a little too messy. For those of us who don't like "messy," this can be a significant obstacle in the journey toward living out your WHY.

That is why I need you to make a conscious decision with me right now. Every single time you believe something you do, say or create has to be "perfect" before you can send it out into the world, promise me that you'll remember that it will NEVER be perfect (nor should it be), and delaying until it's perfect means you'll essentially be deferring your dreams for an entire lifetime.

Maybe you want to have a perfect sounding WHY that makes everyone *ooh* and *aah* when they hear it. But that isn't what matters. What matters is that it truly represents what you believe.

Your WHY doesn't have to fit anyone else's standards. Your WHY is as unique and special as you are. So write it out. Then rewrite it if you need to as you become clearer on your WHY and how to pursue it.

**Remember, you live out your "I believe" in every job, situation and season of life. It will help you to navigate and guide how you work, act and where you go next.

Perfect is boring. In fact, I don't even want this book to stay perfect. I want you to rip out a page of this book right now. Just rip it right out. After you have defined your WHY and written it out back on page 65, I want you to tear it out of this book.

Feels kind of good, doesn't it?

Now, I want you to hang that torn out page where you will see it most. Whether that is on the mirror in your bathroom, the wall in your bedroom, your locker at school or somewhere in your car. You can even take a picture of your WHY statement and make it the background on your phone and computer.

I also recommend that you create a vision board. A vision board is any sort of board on which you display images that represent whatever you want to accomplish or have in your life. The most effective way to make one is to find images and words that represent your WHY and put them together onto a poster board. Then you will hang this board in a location where you will see it multiple times a day.

If this seems a little overboard, I'll let you in on another big secret—you can't obsess *enough* over your WHY.

You need to see it and say it... Every. Single. Day. The more you see it, the more it becomes something you think about. The more you think about it the more likely you are to live it out each and every day of your life.

The more your brain sees your WHY, the more you'll find out how to do things that align with that WHY and learn how to live it out each day.

Living Outside the Matrix

Everyone's WHY is different, and there is certainly no ranking them. There can also be no wrong WHY. Neither your WHY nor my WHY is better or worse than anyone else's.

Be OK with uniqueness. Be OK with being you.

This can be incredibly hard in a society that is overflowing with comparison, judgment and jealousy. We are constantly judging ourselves based on staged photos, photo shopped media images, and perfect looking lives. We allow other people to define whom we are and what we were meant to do because it feels safer than owning and being proud of the person you were *actually* created to be.

> "Always be a first-rate version of yourself, instead of a second-rate version of somebody else."
> *–Judy Garland*

The ironic part is that you will be so much more respected and loved when you are just the real, authentic *you*—and not when you are trying to be someone else whom you think people will prefer.

We waste so many years in our youth trying to measure up to what we think our friends and peers expect of us instead of being brave enough to remove the mask and unapologetically say, "Hey! This is who I am. If you like me—great. If you don't like me—great."

Maybe it stems from being the youngest in my family, or from my naturally independent and rebellious spirit, but nowadays, after a long journey of caring way too much, I just don't care what other people think about me.

I really don't.

Of course, it wasn't always that way. What people thought about me meant FAR too much when I was younger. I lived for having a ton of friends and getting approval. What a waste of my valuable time!

I've changed my perspective so much, and today I am happy and content in the fact that I am totally different from the rest of the world.

My friend Jess Connolly calls this freedom "living outside the Matrix."

For those of you who have never seen the 1999 movie starring Keanu Reeves, *The Matrix* represents the average person's sphere of reality (day-to-day life, the daily grind, whatever you want to call it). It's a set of rules that govern societal expectations, and no one ever lives outside those rules or questions them.

In essence, when you live inside the Matrix, you don't know what you don't know—and you never want to find out. It's a life of blissful (or not so blissful) ignorance. No growth. No change. Just... existing according to rules that someone else made.

Our version of living within the Matrix is spending hours a day on social media, cyber stalking other people's "perfect" lives and trying to craft our own to appear perfect on the screen as well.

You have the choice to join in that insanity OR make your own rules and live outside the Matrix.

What will you choose?

Be different. *Own* your crazy. Dance wildly to your favorite song in the car. Belly laugh until you cry in your local coffee shop. Share your heart and be real to serve others. Love until it hurts and no matter how many times you get stepped on, never stop being you.

Because you, my dear friend, are so awesome.

We don't tell each other enough how special each one of us is, how each of us matter and can impact the world. So, I'm saying this to you from the deepest part of my heart:

You are enough.

You are loved.

You are unique.

You are purposed.

You were created with intention and purpose.

You are changing the world for good.

You are made for so much more than you think you are.

I mean those words. They are not clichéd to me, nor are they filler words. My heart fills when I say these things to others— and here is my challenge to you: Right now, put this book down and go tell someone else that they are enough. Tell a friend, a stranger, a parent, or a teacher that he or she is loved.

Imagine if every single day, we told just **one** person how amazing and unique he or she is. Imagine our world if we started speaking the life-giving truth that, "You are enough just as you are. You were beautifully and intentionally created to live a full, vibrant and impactful life."

I mean it! Go speak truth to someone who needs to hear it.

Defining Your WHY

Welcome back! How did that feel? Could you do that every day? I hope so. That one simple act can change the course of a person's day, maybe their week, maybe even their month. Then think about what would happen if that person did the same for someone else! Your reach would multiply exponentially, and you could be responsible for helping countless others escape their own Matrix.

Whatever you need to do to remind yourself to make this a daily activity, do it. Put a reminder note next to your vision board or on the dash of your car. Set a notification on your phone. Write it on your hand. Whatever it takes.

Be intentional with your words and use them to speak truth and build up those around you. This is one of the simplest and easiest ways to change your school, your community, your town and your world.

You can't lead others without knowing why you were put on this Earth; because if you don't know **why** you want to lead, you won't know **where** or **who** to lead. It would be like trying to hike Mt. Everest for the first time with no plan, no guide and none of the proper tools.

Your WHY may take some time to figure out—and that's normal. It's absolutely OK if you don't know what it is right away.

Take some time to think about it. If you are having trouble, talk it out with a close, trusted friend. Brainstorm about your gifts, your passions, and what excites you. If it is hard for you to think of yourself in that way, ask a trusted friend or family member in what areas you excel. Sometimes others can see our natural gifts and talents better than we can see them.

As you are finding that WHY, there are three questions that must also be answered along the way when it comes to fulfilling your role as a *servant leader*:

WHY? WHO? HOW?

WHY you are going to serve?
WHO you are going to serve?
HOW you are going to serve them?

For example, if your purpose—your big WHY—is to be a teacher, then the **WHO** is your students! And **WHY** are you going to serve those students? You are going to serve them because you want them to grow and find their own WHYS in life. **HOW** are you going to serve them? There could be countless ways, but most importantly, you are going to love on them and show them through your time and actions that you believe in them and will do whatever it takes to support their dreams.

My best friend is an art teacher at a local school in Pittsburgh.

Her **WHY** in life is to make an impact through teaching and creating art.

Her **WHO** is all of her art students.

Her **HOW** is the way she teaches, how she deals with conflict, and the ways she pushes her students to be better artists and leaders.

One of the best ways she pushes them is through an "Encouragement Wall" that she created. This is a wall outside her art room that has multiple boxes in which any student can reach and grab a little note of encouragement.

She has taught her art students to not only be encouraged by those notes, but to also leave multiple notes of encouragement in the boxes to help other students in their school.

Now, she is impacting the students in her class as well as all of the students throughout her school by encouraging and challenging those in her art classes.

When you act for the sake of something other than personal recognition, fame, money, glory, or out of obligation, your WHY will help you defy the odds and affect change when it seems impossible to others.

Your WHY is the foundation on which you can build whatever change you wish to see in the world. You have the ability to see that change become reality, and all it requires is your action.

Three Pieces to the WHY Puzzle

As you remember **WHO** you are serving, **WHY** you are serving and **HOW** you are going to serve, let's break the word WHY down even more.

We versus Me

Hang tough when you've had enough

You are the glue

Take your time and study these three principles; they will be the focus of the rest of the book. Here is why they are everything:

- When you remember **WHO** you are serving, you remember that it isn't about you; it's about the collective **we** rather than the individual **me**. It's about all the people you are called to serve and impact.

- When you remember *WHY* you are serving, you can stick through the hard times—you can **hang tough** when you've had enough—and keep coming back to why you started in the beginning.

- When you remember *HOW* you are serving, it comes back to you doing something and becoming the **glue** that holds your plan together. You have to start being the impact before anyone can actually be impacted.

Again, I may not know you personally, but I already know what you're thinking—and I get it. I have felt that way, too. Your Mt. Everest problem is looming over you and your WHY doesn't seem good enough or big enough to overcome what's ahead of you.

So, it's best to give up now before you just let others down, right? Maybe someone else will come along who's better, smarter or more talented than you and tackle this big problem with much more style and skill.

Sure, maybe someone who fits that description will come along. But how much worse will the issue be one, five, or ten years down the road?

By that time, you'll look back and realize that ignoring your WHY caused you to live a mediocre life of semi-influence rather than an extraordinary life of immense influence and impact.

Let's look at someone who I admire greatly, someone who had an overwhelming and seemingly unsolvable Mt. Everest problem that plenty of other people shared. But something separated this man from everyone else in overcoming the mountain.

The difference?

His WHY.

Martin Luther King, Jr. had a problem that many people wanted to fix and tried to fix, but with not much success.

Something big had to bring millions of people together to unite them under a single, shared vision: Racial equality.

King achieved an unprecedented accomplishment when he gathered a quarter of a million people together to march on Washington D.C. on August 28th, 1963. He spoke from his WHY—he truly had a dream. Here are just a few excerpts from his moving "I Have a Dream" speech, delivered on that day at the Lincoln Memorial:

> *"...I have a dream that one day this nation will rise up and live out the true meaning of its creed: 'We hold these truths to be self-evident, that all men are created equal'...*
>
> *...I have a dream that my four little children will one day live in a nation where they will not be judged by the color of their skin but by the content of their character...*
>
> *I have a dream today!*
>
> *I have a dream that one day every valley shall be exalted, and every hill and mountain shall be made low, the rough places will be made plain, and the crooked places will be made straight; 'and the glory of the Lord shall be revealed and all flesh shall see it together.'*
>
> *This is our hope, and this is the faith that I go back to the South with.*
>
> *With this faith, we will be able to hew out of the mountain of despair a stone of hope. With this faith, we will be able to transform the jangling discords of our nation into a*

beautiful symphony of brotherhood. With this faith, we will be able to work together, to pray together, to struggle together, to go to jail together, to stand up for freedom together, knowing that we will be free one day..."

Martin Luther King Jr. didn't say, "Hey everyone, pull it together! Let's get over this." He also didn't sit back and complain about how bad things were.

He did something.

He stood up, united a nation and spoke from his WHY—and that WHY coupled with his own actions and the actions of those who followed him have changed our nation forever.

No matter the size of your Mt. Everest problem or how many people seem to be trying to solve it, *your* WHY and *your* talents and gifts can change the world forever.

When Goals are Useless

I'm tired of hearing about goals.

You know why?

Goals mean nothing if you don't have your WHY.

When life gets hard, when things are tough, when you don't want to keep moving forward, goals won't help. They won't push you to keep fighting and keep moving no matter what knocks you down. No matter what life throws at you, who tries to tear you down or how impossible this journey seems, it's your WHY that will get you to keep going.

Goals are useless without a strong WHY.

The real problem with goals lies in the fact that often we make goals based on other people's expectations, our own unrealistic expectations, or what we *think* we should be doing. Then one day, you look up and find that you have reached your goals and yet you aren't where you want to be, and you aren't doing what you want to be doing.

It is so easy to get distracted by other opportunities that come our way or the opinions of others in our lives. Luckily, finding your WHY can keep you from getting distracted and setting the wrong goals that will lead you down unintended paths. Your WHY will help steer your goals in the right direction; and when you start to get off track, your WHY will be there to remind you to stick to the right path.

Think of your WHY like guardrails on the highway. Those rails are there to keep you from driving off a cliff. Your WHY is much the same; it serves as a great boundary to keep you on the path for which you were created.

It's time to stop giving other people permission to dictate our lives. We hand over our identity, our talents, and our gifts and let everyone else decide what to do with them. But if those things are not in line with your WHY, they aren't right for you.

Become the guardian of your WHY. Don't let anyone take it from you, tear it down or tell you differently. Protect it, and it will guide you where you ultimately want to be.

"Your WHY is your permission slip to live out your boldest, wildest life dreams that leave a legacy and impacts those around you."

—*Anni Keffer*

5

<u>W</u>e Versus Me

TODAY'S LEADERS ARE a lot like islands.

They are the figureheads of companies and those people in the public eye, many of whom have had tremendous personal success and were placed into a leadership position because of that success.

Their role as leader was awarded to them primarily because of what they accomplished. They "stepped up" and became leaders because they were expected to, or because they wanted to achieve even greater heights in their careers.

This has become the normal way of thinking about leadership, but the truth is: it's just not working anymore. Why? Because in its current form, the idea of "stepping up and being a leader" means that you need to be *above* other people and tell them where to go.

You're in charge and everyone follows *your* command.

But here's the truth—leadership isn't about you. It's not about the individual "ME." It's about the collective "WE." The entire point of servant leadership is to serve people in what you believe, which is why the question you should always ask yourself is:

How do I get out of my own way and help others get to where <u>they</u> want to go?

Here's the really great (and ironic) secret waiting to be revealed. When you serve those in your season of life, doing what you believe and help them achieve more than you and they thought possible, you actually get further in *your* life.

This may seems backwards, but servant leadership is the only type of leadership that lasts; in fact, it will carry you from now until your last day on earth.

That is why I'm boldly calling you to rise up and claim the role of servant leader by putting those who fit into your WHY *above* yourself.

This is a bold ask—and I get that. It's daring partly because there is so much to overcome. We first have to get past some seriously engrained ideas that are as much a part of our culture as are baseball and apple pie. So, take a deeper look at some of those ideas.

Leadership from the Bottom

Right now, there are leaders across this nation and all over the world that are leading from the top. That type of leadership looks like this:

With this traditional form of leadership, everyone is under you. You tell them what to do, where to go and how to get there. There is not much connection, value or relationship building with this type of leadership. You don't push or challenge those under you to be better or to grow, and they don't push you to be a better leader.

A better term for what you are doing is "manager" rather than "leader."

Top-down leadership is fine if you want to make no lasting impact and don't want to see anything in this world change for the better.

In contrast...

With servant leadership, you are on the bottom and everyone you are serving is above you. You are pushing them to be better, to grow, to challenge the status quo, and they challenge you to be a better leader for them and for others.

Regardless of where you are in life right now, if you believe you are being called to be a leader, servant leadership will allow you to have the greatest impact on a local and global scale. Seth Godin calls this kind of world-changing pioneer a "Linchpin Leader," and he defines such a person like this:

Linchpin Leader:

"A human being who is doing original, brave work; a person who we would have trouble living without. Somebody whom we would miss if they were gone."

If you want to be that kind of leader, there are some important areas of your life that must be defined before you can become a trailblazer that the world can't be without.

Unfortunately, like "leader," the words "purpose" and "mission" have also reached buzzword status, which lessens their impact. So let's take a moment to define these terms at their most fundamental level so you can internalize them and then begin honing in on your WHY if you are still attempting to define it in your life.

Your Purpose:
The reason for which you were created.

Your *purpose* is what some might call "the meaning of life." It's the big question that many people spend a lifetime trying to determine but never seem to figure out. It's more general than your mission, and defining your purpose will help *lead* you to your mission.

Your Mission:
What you are called to do as a
result of knowing your purpose.

Your mission is the action you are going to take as a result of your purpose. It is the manifestation of your purpose. It's what Gandhi meant by "BEing" the change.

Because so many of the people around you exist without ever defining their purpose, they are also unable to define their mission. *Doesn't it make so much sense now that so many people are unhappy?* Without knowing your purpose and therefore your mission in life, it robs life of its meaning and makes our actions seem routine, commonplace, and uninspired.

Yes, I realize these are high-level concepts; but they are also fundamental truths about your life that most people (and maybe even your family and close friends) don't know about you. And maybe, just maybe, you have yet to define them for yourself.

Now is the time!

Back in Chapter 4, I asked you to define your WHY. Since the concept of defining a WHY may still be new to you, we will break it down even further into its two pieces. Your WHY is your *mission* and your *purpose*, simply stated, in a way that compels you to keep moving forward. And so, define the following:

My Purpose is:

_____

_____

_____

_____

My Mission is:

_____

_____

_____

Then, combine your purpose and your mission to make your WHY. (You can write the same WHY you did back in chapter 4, or you can reword it now that you have better defined your purpose and your mission):

My purpose and mission-driven WHY is:

_____

_____

_____

A good, simplified example of a possible purpose and mission (your WHY) might be:

"My purpose is to help children flourish in this world, and therefore my mission is to provide a better education to as many children as possible."

These two things combine to form your WHY, which might then compel you to **act** by becoming a teacher, a missionary, a nonprofit worker overseas, or simply a volunteer on the weekends at the local library to help teach kids how to read.

Each and every one of those callings, whether full-time or part-time, is noble and brave. **You can change the world on the weekends!** Why not? You can do anything you want to do if your WHY is strong enough!

If you can't define your purpose and mission (aka your WHY) right away, don't worry. Just answer them the best you can, and I promise you, by the time you finish this book, you will be able to give yourself permission to look deep into your heart and honestly find the answers you seek.

Ready to Remove the Mask?

Speaking of honesty, do you want to know a secret about me? I was once the queen of masks. For years, people have only gotten to know the version of me that I'm willing to put on display.

I have spent much of my life covering up my heart and my real identity so people can't get to know the *real* me.

Because of my desire to hide the real me, I tried my best to get to know everyone else on a deeper level. I learned that by keeping all the questions focused on others and what they were going through, no one had the opportunity to turn the tables and open *me* up for scrutiny.

This massive cover-up agenda came from a place of fear. It always felt too scary to let people in to see me and my gifts, passions, and dreams. In fact, I even convinced myself that I was selfish for wanting to talk about my dreams for the future.

Ironically, what I didn't realize was that I was actually being even more selfish (and a tad arrogant) by not allowing anyone to really see into my passions and desires for the future and let them know what I desperately wanted to change in the world. I didn't realize that talking about these things would actually *help* me in the journey to lead and to affect change rather than hurt it.

Then I remembered my Mt. Everest problem: I wanted to expose the lie that we are never enough. And how was I going to fix that problem? By BEING the change I so desperately wished to see in the world.

My ability to change the world started with me—and it starts with you.

The first step on your leadership journey is the brave act of removing the mask you may have created to keep people from seeing who you really are and replacing your mask with openness, authenticity and vulnerability.

That's a pretty scary thought, isn't it? Being daring enough to let people see who you truly are is one of the most tremendously courageous things you can do.

What image have you put out into the world that doesn't really represent who you are? Do your social media pages paint a perfect picture of your life? How often do you have conversations with acquaintances and even good friends that feel like "just another surface conversation?" These are all signs you have been wearing a mask.

You, your relationships, your school and your world can be completely transformed with the one simple act of taking off that mask. Because the truth is, the world will never change if all we are focused on is making sure people think that we never make mistakes, we never fail, and we have it all together.

We have this overwhelming tendency to want to make our lives look like some Cinderella fairytale with magic, fairy godmothers, Prince Charmings and happily ever afters—and we leave out the failures, sadness and dreams of living a life different than the one we have.

This is done so much in social media. Instead of using online platforms to lead courageously, we hide behind a beautifully crafted façade that keeps others just out of reach.

The bravery comes in knowing that no one is served by your fictitious fairytale; they can only be served by your honesty.

Leaders speak their story openly with an understanding that if one person was helped by it, it was worth it because remember, it's not about "me"... it's about "we." It is the world changers who are willing to be transparent, those who are willing to share their messy, imperfect lives.

I continue to learn this lesson, even as I write this book. That is because as easy as it would be for me to tell you, "I have arrived" and "look at all my success now," that wouldn't be helpful to you, nor would it paint a complete and comprehensive picture of my life so far.

I share, instead, from a place of vulnerability and from having walked through different seasons in my life, failing a lot along the way, gaining wisdom through it and now sharing my experiences with you. I am not perfect, nor will I ever be. My journey will continue to hit road blocks, and I'll no doubt continue to fail and get back up, learning more about myself and my WHY with each disappointment and recovery.

It's not easy to share those things about myself and to walk away from the pointless pursuit of perfection, but if you take at least one thing away from this book, it was all worth it.

So do something with me, will you?

Let's revisit this idea of "perfection" from the last chapter by performing a little exercise I learned from my friend, Julie Carrier. Ready?

THROW PERFECTION OUT THE DOOR!

Instructions:

Rip out this page and
throw it out of the door
closest to you.

How did that feel?

My hope is that when you look back on this book and see the remnants of that ripped out page, you'll remember that perfection and the attempt to act or be seen as perfect has been thrown out of your life.

During my own struggles with perfectionism my friend Julie Carrier shared this tactic with me. It felt totally bizarre, but it helped me to have a visual picture of what to do when I feel the urge to put on the mask of perfection.

Once you've cleared the way for perfection to be thrown aside (right where it belongs) and allow vulnerability and authenticity into your life, you can focus on what the real pursuit of leadership looks like: Finding your WHY, and then serving the people within that WHY.

Right now, you might be thinking, "Easier said than done, Anni."

Believe me, I know—and despite the fact that deep down, we know we will never be perfect, we all continue to strive for perfection, don't we? To achieve it all, be it all, do it all. But here is the real underlying problem with perfection:

It is that attempt to achieve perfection that keeps the focus solely on you not on the people you want to impact. The pointless pursuit of perfection is what makes it about "me" and not about "we."

Perfection in life is simply unattainable, so don't worry about the critics; because the real supporters, the real mentors in your life, they aren't critics. They aren't the people who regularly comment on your work and your dreams just because they think they should or just because they love the sound of their own voice.

Mentors are those walking beside and ahead of you, doing brave work and leading with their *own* WHY; they are pushing you to always grow.

Lead Like Somebody's Watching

Despite what we've been led to believe, leadership isn't about being outgoing, popular or super knowledgeable about a particular subject. In fact, leadership in its purest form is simple:

LEADERSHIP =

Discovering your WHY and leading out what you believe in every area, in every season, and with everyone you meet.

It's simple, but that doesn't mean it's easy. This is why it is possible that right now, you may not feel equipped; you may feel worthless or have been told you're worthless; you may even feel you don't have a WHY.

All of those things you've been led to believe are lies; they are lies meant to hold you back from finding what you are called to do and doing it right now (not doing it once you graduate college, or gain enough experience or are told you are now *allowed* to pursue your passion).

Leadership built on WHY is about starting right now, where you are, and with who you are and what you know, while always being ready to learn and grow more, fail and get back up to move forward.

Want to know why you should start today?

Because leaders are not born; they're made.

That means that anyone can *become* a leader! And guess who gets to decide whether or not you are going to become one—you! Perhaps even more importantly, you are also in charge of the kind of leader you want to be.

How so?

1. First, you get to choose to whom you will listen. Who will you allow into your circle of influence? What do you allow the people closest to you to put into your life through their words, priorities, beliefs, passions, opinions, and actions?

2. Second, you have the choice to read books, find mentors and coaches, listen to podcasts, and watch videos that will help equip you to be the leader you know you can be and want to be.

My hope is that this book becomes the catalyst you need to take the first step and remove the mask so that your focus can become, "***Who can I help***?" instead of "***How can I help myself***?"

For me, a young woman named Emily became one of the biggest reminders of why "WE instead of ME" is so powerful when it comes to being a leader. Do you have a certain person in your life that instantly makes you smile when you see him or her? Emily is one of those people who lights up a room when she enters it.

Emily attends my church and is a member of the youth group where I volunteer on Wednesday nights. She is a beautiful, kind, quiet girl who has a deep passion for Jesus and acts as a leader wherever she goes.

During her senior year in high school, Emily came up to me one Wednesday night and told me something for which I was completely unprepared. She was taking a speech class, and the final speech was supposed to be about someone who inspired her.

She had chosen *me.*

Say what?? Come again, girlfriend? I must not have heard you right.

There is no way anyone could have written a speech about me, but it happened—and it profoundly impacted who I am and how I navigate leading and impacting.

You never know who is watching you and how you are changing lives around you... just by being you. So lead every day of your life like people are watching—because they are!

After all, it's all about them anyway.

"*Fail* is not a four-letter word; it's simply proof that you're trying."

—*Anni Keffer*

6

Hang Tough When You've Had Enough

Spoiler Alert:

After you define your WHY, and begin down the path of servant leadership, you are going to feel a strong, at times uncontrollable, urge to give up.

Maybe next week, maybe next year, maybe five years from now (and maybe at every point in between), there will be moments where you would rather quit than keep going. The urge to call it quits will come and go, vary in length, and will happen for lots of reasons.

Finding the WHY that compels you forward and gives you the fuel you need to envision changing the world isn't an instant cure for disappointment, nor is it a free pass to instantaneous happiness and fulfillment.

Sometimes nothing will be working...and everyone will seem to be against you.

That is called life—and all of those experiences and feelings are completely normal.

You aren't crazy and you aren't alone.

THAT'S A TOUGH pill to swallow, isn't it? So why even bother?

Isn't understanding your passions supposed to make life more fulfilling?

Well, let me put it this way. Have you ever accomplished a great feat? Maybe you excelled at a certain sport, got all A's in school, or saved every dime you ever made and bought your own new car.

What is the one thing all of those accomplishments have in common? They weren't easy!

And here's another spoiler alert for you: Nothing in life worth having ever is.

So how do you fight the urge to quit? You can overcome the inclination by always coming back to your WHY—by coming back to the reason you started leading in the first place—

> "A lot of what is most beautiful about the world arises from struggle."
>
> *—Malcolm Gladwell*

because the truth is, leadership will be lonely from time to time.

You won't always be the most liked person when you stand for something, and undoubtedly, there will be others who will be jealous or feel insecure about the strides you're making in your life.

Sometimes, you will be called to stand up when everyone else sits down. Sometimes, you will called to be the one who walks left when everyone else walks right. Neither of those callings is something you'll want to face, but going back to your WHY will help you do it with conviction and resolve.

"Things don't go wrong and break your heart so you can become bitter and give up. They happen to break you down and build you up so you can be all that you were intended to be."
—*Charlie Jones*

Are You Whale Shark Enough?

Another side effect of pursuing your WHY is encountering an ugly thing called *criticism*. Don't like criticism? No one does. But you're gonna need to get used to it—and then get over it. Even better, go ahead and become a whale shark. Here's a picture of one:

Whale sharks are the largest fish in the sea, and thankfully for us humans, they prefer plankton to meat. Now, I'm guessing you've probably never been told to be like a whale shark before. So what does that really have to do with leadership?

Whale sharks have *insanely* thick skin—like four inches thick. Just think about how dense that is for a minute. That's just about how thick a wall in your house is; that skin is no joke.

This thick layer of skin comes in pretty handy for the whale shark. When a whale shark is swimming around minding its own business or pursuing its whale shark passion in life (which I assume is to eat plankton) and an ocean predator tries to attack it, the whale shark's skin keeps the bad out... and the good in.

You need to be like that whale shark; you have got to have thick skin. When people criticize, laugh at, or bully you for what you're doing, you have to keep the bad out and the good in.

People tend to criticize what they don't understand, what threatens them or what makes them feel jealous, and at many different points along the way, you and your actions will cause people to feel all those emotions.

It happens—but you have to keep it from deterring you from your mission and purpose. So, be like that whale shark.

This is also the reason your WHY is so critical! When you have one of those days when you don't feel like forging ahead—maybe someone mocked you, called you a stupid dreamer,

> "If you aren't upsetting someone, you aren't changing the status quo."
> —*Seth Godin*

or just stared at you like you were crazy—you look at your WHY, say it out loud, and just keep on keepin' on.

Remember that when others criticize who you are and what you're doing, it's not a reflection on you. They are really just speaking out of their own insecurities rather than speaking truths about you.

Here's the best part about being criticized (as if you ever thought there was a best part): it means that you're doing something. Creating waves of change that will shake up the status quo will catch the attention of naysayers.

Truthfully, it is those very moments that make you a stronger and better leader. Such moments also show those around you that nothing this world throws at you can come between you and your WHY.

> "Someone's opinion of you does not have to become your reality."
> —*Les Brown*

Habits: Easy to Form, Hard to Break

I don't care if you're a guy or a girl; there is one thing we all have in common: We all struggle with negative self-talk. On the daily, we tell ourselves lies about our failures, our appearance, and our abilities. We imprint these negative untruths on our brains, day in and day out until guess what?

Your brain decides to start believing them as truths.

Your brain is like a computer; you can program it to do and believe anything that you want...both the good and the bad.

And the more you do any specific action or repeat or think anything consistently, the more engrained in you it becomes.

And *that* is the basic explanation for how habits and belief systems are formed.

As a simplistic example, when you were young, your parents probably taught you to brush your teeth twice a day. You continually repeated this same action twice a day, year after year, and it eventually became a habit that you didn't need to think about anymore. Somewhere along the way, brushing your teeth became as much an automatic part of your life as breathing or eating.

This same principle applies to anything in your life. If you continually say or do the same thing, every single day, it will become a normal practice that can influence you to do and be better—or it can be greatly destructive.

Habits can be formed even more easily than that. You can start doing something just casually (on the weekends only perhaps) that can eventually turn into an every day kind of thing.

Let's say you start going to parties with your friends because you feel the pressure to fit in and be a part of the in-crowd. You start going to parties every once in a while, drinking here and there, and you only mildly enjoy the experience each time. It's not really your scene, but you keep going.

After a while, you start to become someone the "cool kids" say hi to more often. You start to feel *seen* rather than continue to feel like you must be wearing some cloak of invisibility.

So what happens? You eventually become a person who parties every weekend. Deep down you realize that the partying and drinking isn't worth it, but it's become a habit.

You're addicted to the social results—and the longer it goes on, the harder it is to break the habit.

Negative self-talk can produce the same, habit-forming negative results. If you call yourself *ugly* when you look in the mirror, *stupid* when you don't do well on a test, or *horrible* when you mess up in a game—and you do it continually—not only will this turn into a habit, but you'll begin to believe every word.

It will also be nearly impossible to believe anyone's compliment or praise about you, and you'll be stuck in the vicious cycle of self-hatred and negativity.

This is the power we have over ourselves; we have this brain-training ability that we can use for making our lives and the lives of those around us better or worse. You must decide to harness this ability for the good. If you don't, then you'll almost certainly succumb to criticism, and when the going gets tough, you will throw in the towel every time.

Garbage In, Garbage Marinates, Garbage Infects

What does your brain believe about you right now, in this moment? Do you feel like no one sees you, pays attention to anything you do, or even cares that you are here? Do you think you're invisible?

If you think or have ever though such things, then know this: They are _all lies_ your negative self-talk has programmed your brain, over time, to believe as truths.

No one is invisible. I mean that—no one.

And even if you don't consider yourself to be one of the "popular" or "cool" kids, people are still watching you.

Remember in the last chapter when I asked you to "lead like somebody's watching?" I said that because at *any* given time and on *any* given day, your friends, family, teachers, and even random people at school or work are paying attention to your behavior.

You take up space on this earth, and whether or not you believe it yet, you are leaving imprints on this planet everywhere you go. People notice how you treat yourself, how you treat others, how you view the world, and the way you act. ***That is why the smallest habits you choose to start and the things you say about yourself have the ability to influence those around us.***

Don't believe me? That's okay. I wouldn't have believed that a few years ago either. My dad would continually tell me that I was a leader and that people paid attention to what I did, and of course, as a know-it-all 17 year old, I thought this was complete nonsense.

That is, until one day in my senior year in high school during physics class.

Enrolling in an honors physics class was probably about THE worst decision I could have ever made that year. Not only am I not what you would consider a "science-y" person, but also I didn't realize what horrible affliction would soon overtake me.

You all know what I'm talking about; it's an epidemic that sweeps across graduating classes across America. It was an illness called "Senioritis," and man, it hit me hard. About half way through the year, I stopped caring. I generally don't recommend that you stop caring about your classes, especially as a senior, but let's be real—it happens to a lot of us.

So there I was, sitting in a class I had no business taking that year, doing lab work at the black top lab tables that encompassed the room. On this particular day, as I was trying hard to concentrate on my work, something slipped and fell, taking me by surprise and causing me to do something I never did:

I swore quite loudly.

Some of you might be laughing to yourselves right now, thinking this isn't a big deal. And just so you know, I was not some goody two-shoes who never did anything wrong. Swearing was simply something I didn't do. It wasn't me being "better" than everyone else—it was a personal choice I had made because of my faith.

Well, as soon as it slipped out, my eyes grew huge, my face glowed bright red and my mouth slammed to the floor. I was mortified.

More than that, I couldn't believe what my lab partner said next.

"I'm so proud of you!" she exclaimed. "You finally swore!"

Proud of me? Did she really just say that?

That experience brought about two key revelations for me. First, it really hit home that even if you don't think people are paying attention to what you do and don't say and do, they are. They're always watching.

Second, I realized that I was surrounded by people who constantly swore, and my mind had soaked in their own use of expletives more than I realized. After my brain had been marinating in those words for long enough, one of them finally came out.

You've probably heard the phrase, "Garbage In, Garbage Out." Well, in my experience, there is no immediate garbage in, garbage out.

It's more like, "Garbage In, Garbage Marinates, and then the Garbage comes out and infects."

That is why after you have consistently filled your brain with garbage such as, "I'm ugly and fat," or "No one likes me," or "I am a failure," that crap will saturate your brain, and you will act as though those lies are true.

And as a result, you will make decisions in all aspects of your life based upon lies!

It is rare that our friends or family know about this internal garbage we allow to fester, but nonetheless, these words, thoughts and ideas intensify until they either stop us when the going gets tough or keep us from taking the first step altogether.

Decide that today is the day you start looking at yourself in the mirror and loving what you see, both inside and out. You don't have to change a single thing about you to love you TODAY.

What Words Are You Wearing?

I'm an extremely visual person. Seeing is believing for me.

So when I talk at high schools and middle schools, colleges, events, and youth groups, I like to find ways to help my audience *visualize* leadership. For one particular youth group, I was talking to their girls about identity, beauty, and the struggle we have with accepting and being proud of who we are. I asked them to do the following:

"No one can make you feel inferior without your consent."

—Eleanor Roosevelt

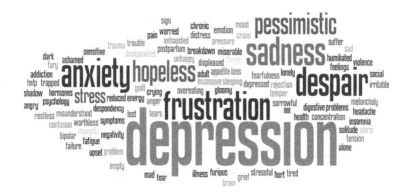

Imagine writing out all of the negative thoughts that you think about yourself on a daily basis, and then picture writing down each individual thought on a notecard. Now imagine taping those words all over your body and going to school covered in those notecards every single day. All of that negativity and self-loathing would be exposed for the world to see as you walk down the halls of your school.

Now imagine writing down on notecards all of the wonderful, true things about you. It's the kind of things your real friends, family and teachers think about you, the wonderful truth. Every day you wake up and you cover yourself in the truth—strong empowering words that make you feel like you can conquer the world—and *that* is what you go to school wearing.

Can you see and *feel* the difference? The girls who did the exercise felt it, too. In fact, Emily, the young lady who did her final speech about me, talked about that activity in her speech:

> *"I remember one time at my youth group, Anni was teaching a lesson on beauty to all the girls. She gave us a visual I still have in my mind. She covered a friend in notecards of comparison. One set of cards was filled with negativity and self-doubt. Those notecards stuck to the person as a label. Anni spoke about how we so often define ourselves as society sees fit, and how we should really define ourselves rather than allow society to do it for us."*

Leaders don't want to blend in; they understand the importance and beauty of standing out. And with that understanding comes the knowledge that living a life of leadership opens you to criticism and ridicule from others.

You're standing up for something greater than yourself, and people won't always like it, but remember: **If people are against you because you're living your purpose, you're doing it right.**

Always consider the source of criticism. People who are willing to criticize you and cut you down more than likely do the same to everyone! My bet is that they are miserable—and misery loves company.

You have to assume the attacks will come, because they will. But you can withstand the attacks by adopting an unquestionable identity based on self-truths rather than lies perpetuated by society.

This is the only way to stay tough when you would have otherwise had enough.

Epic Fails Lead to Epic Success

Failure. Don't you just hate that word?

It stinks; it's terrifying and intimidating. It is one of the biggest influencers in our decision to hang tough or quit when the going gets rough.

The word *failure* is another one of those elephants in the room. Like *perfection*, we all know failure is there; we all fail, but we never want to talk about it, think about it or confront it.

Because of our inability, or more accurately *lack of willingness* to face it, that's when the fear of failure wins. It triumphs and takes over when we allow ourselves to sit in the dark places of our minds and grow more powerful because we pretend it's not there rather than confront it.

That is why you better believe that's what we're going to do—confront it and kick it squarely in the face. We are going to do this because here's the real deal:

Failure is actually awesome, because it's the only path to becoming truly successful.

I know that some of you just reread that line a few times to make sure you read that correctly.

Yes, friends, failure is the bomb.

I've failed a million times, and yet I'm still alive, still being a leader, and still accomplishing success. In fact, you can't even achieve success without proper failure.

Want proof?

Albert Einstein. Most of us take Einstein's name as synonymous with genius, but his road was paved with *nothing* but failure. Einstein did not even speak until he was four and did not read until he was seven, causing his teachers and parents to think he was mentally handicapped, slow and socially inept. Eventually, he was expelled from school and was refused admittance to the Zurich Polytechnic School. With that much failure and negativity, isn't it amazing that the boy who everyone thought was mentally challenged went on to win the Nobel Prize and change the face of modern physics!

Oprah Winfrey. We know Oprah as one of the most iconic faces on TV as well as one of the richest and most successful women in the world. Oprah faced a hard road to get to that position, however, enduring a rough and often abusive childhood as well as numerous career setbacks including being fired from her job as a television reporter because she was "unfit for TV." Oprah? Unfit for TV?

Bill Gates. We all know Microsoft and its billionaire founder Mr. Gates. But did you also know that he dropped out of Harvard to start a failed first business with Microsoft co-founder Paul Allen called Traf-O-Data?

> "Failure is an event, never a person."
>
> —*William D. Brown*

Elvis Presley. As one of the best-selling music artists of all time, Elvis is a worldwide icon. But back in 1954, Elvis was still a nobody, and Jimmy Denny, manager of the Grand Ole Opry, fired Elvis Presley after just one performance telling him, "You ain't goin' nowhere, son. You ought to go back to drivin' a truck."

Those are just a few examples of the countless number of world changers who failed over and over again.

Still don't believe that failure is the bomb? Let's look at this from a different perspective. Take Sara Blakely, the founder of Spanx. When she and her brother were growing up, every night at the dinner table her dad would ask them how they failed that day.

(I'm serious.)

> "The secret of being wrong isn't to avoid being wrong! The secret is being willing to be wrong...
> The desire to fail on the way to reaching a bigger goal is the untold secret of success."
> —*Seth Godin*

If they had not failed, he would ask them to go out and fail and then tell him about it the next day.

You know what that did?

For Sara, it completely removed *all* fear of failing. Failing became such a normal part of life that it helped her pursue big dreams and goals because when she failed, at any point, she knew she could keep getting better and stronger.

That's what you and I have to choose every day; we need to see failure as a good thing and not something to avoid at all costs.

The problem is that we tend to look at people who are wildly successful and believe that they got there overnight. We either pass over or don't realize all of the failures that got them to where they are today; just as I'm sure most people do when they think of people like Oprah and Elvis.

We paint a pretty, perfect picture of their success, and when we don't do it as "quickly" as they did, we call ourselves failures. If only we could pull back the curtain on their real lives and see that those we idolize had a ton of failure before they reached success; and more than that, even now that they are succeeding,

> ## "Part of leadership (a big part of it, actually) is the ability to stick with the dream for a long time. Long enough that the critics realize that you're going to get there one way or another...so they follow."
> ### *—Seth Godin*

they still have their fair share of failures and mistakes.

The name Walt Disney is certainly known for all his success, right? It's hard to imagine anyone more successful. I believed for a long time that he must have just been in the "right place at the right time" and did all the right things.

Wrong.

Walt Disney was fired in 1919 from his job at a newspaper because he apparently "lacked imagination and had no good ideas."

After that, Disney started a number of businesses that didn't last too long and ended with bankruptcy and failure, including a failed animation studio.

He kept plugging along, however, and eventually found a recipe for success that worked. He went on to form the Walt Disney Company, the empire that has touched and inspired billions all around the world.

If you think about it, would Walt Disney have been able to create his household brand into what it is today if he hadn't been fired and landed a company in bankruptcy? No way! He needed to fail in order to be pushed to be better and to learn what *not* to do and then what he *should* be doing.

I had my own big moment of public failure—a moment of failure in front of 600 people, to be exact. The summer after my freshman year of college, I was a counselor at a teen summer camp.

For eight weeks out of the summer, we lived on what was called the Island, and it WAS a legitimate island, meaning you had to take a boat to get on and off the property. So I appropriately named it Alcatraz (for those of you who don't recognize that name, it's an old prison off the coast of San Francisco that is surrounded by water).

Looking back, that summer was an amazing time of growth in my life. I encountered situations and people that would help ground me and gain perspective about the world.

It just didn't always feel that way in the moment.

Each day we had chapel in the morning and again at night. During those chapels, they would ask some of the counselors to speak on various topics and briefly share their stories. When they asked me to speak, I was pumped. The opportunity came just a few months after I had figured out my WHY and had decided I wanted to speak and start my own company.

Still on fire about my decision and yet to actually do any real speaking beyond my high school speech class, I had some serious learning to do about my WHY. At the time, I prematurely viewed myself as this big hotshot speaker. So when I got asked to share my story, I couldn't wait to show the entire staff, counselors and all the campers what I had to offer.

These chapels were held in the large stadium seating-style meeting hall with the stage at the front. My girls and I sat in the second row, and as I anxiously waited for my moment to shine, I imagined all these amazing scenarios of how great I was going to do, and my ego was growing bigger than an NBA all-star's.

They called my name, and I walked the five feet down to the bottom of the steps in my orange t-shirt, baggy jeans and blue flip-flops. Ready for my grand debut that was sure to wow the audience, I went to hop up the two feet on the stage in front of me.

Little did I know that my flip-flops would have a different idea about how things should go. As I made my small leap onto the stage, the front of my dirty blue flip-flops caught the edge of the stage, throwing me forward onto my face and thrusting my butt high into the air.

To say that the audience of 600 broke out into laughter would be an understatement... people were *crying* from laughing so hard.

In that instant, I had a choice: I could run off the stage and consider myself a failure (which was tempting to do given my present level of embarrassment), OR I could pick myself up, laugh with the audience (because let's face it, it was pretty funny), swallow my pride, deflate my ego and deliver the same message I had planned to give.

Thankfully I chose the second option—and each of us has the same choice when faced with any kind of failure.

Giving up is easy. Staying the course is brave, because failure, whether in front of an audience of 600 or in your classroom at school, never feels good. In those moments you have to slow down and remember how great —and necessary—failure is in the long run.

As you fail, you are on the path to succeeding! The more no's you hear about an idea, a business, a book, or anything else, the closer you are to someone saying yes.

You just have to learn to be content with persistence.

This is where your WHY will again come into play. Even as you continue to fail, coming back to your WHY will ground you and allow you to remember the whole point. Then you can laugh or cry (whichever makes you feel better) and look at the failure as a great opportunity to learn, grow, try it again or move on to something else.

You know how when you are trying to work up the courage to ask someone on a date, pursue a job or sell something, everyone likes to encourage you by saying, "C'mon, what's the worst that could happen?"

Then we're supposed to say, "They might say no," and that's supposed to help us make the tough ask.

Well, I say that hearing no is sometimes the _best_ thing that could happen!

Sometimes the no's in our lives actually lead us to where we *really* need to go rather than where we *think* we need to go.

I've always loved the line, "If you want to make God laugh, tell Him your plans." Because let's face it—there's not much in life that goes exactly according to how we plan it in our heads. Reality just works that way. So, the next time you hear a no, think of it as God's way of getting you on the right path—and then keep on going.

> "It is impossible to live without failing at something, unless you live so cautiously that you might as well not have lived at all – in which case, you fail by default."
> *—JK Rowling*

"It is not the critic who counts; not the man who points out how the strong man stumbles, or where the doer of deeds could have done them better. The credit belongs to the man who is actually in the arena, whose face is marred by dust and sweat and blood; who strives valiantly; who errs, who comes short again and again, because there is no effort without error and shortcoming; but who does actually strive to do the deeds; who knows great enthusiasms, the great devotions; who spends himself in a worthy cause; who at the best knows in the end the triumph of high achievement, and who at the worst, if he fails, at least fails while daring greatly, so that his place shall never be with those cold and timid souls who neither know victory nor defeat."

—*Theodore Roosevelt*

7

You Are the Glue

"A life isn't significant except for its impact on other lives."

—Jackie Robinson

HOW MANY "ORDINARY" people do you know?

Most of the people who cross our paths in this life come and go without much impact on us or our lives and don't particularly stand out in any unique, lasting way.

It's not that we mean to live ordinary lives.

Ordinary is *safe*, and ordinary doesn't require you to face your fears, define your WHY, swim upstream, upset the status quo, or subject yourself to the ridicule of others.

An ordinary life is one that is lived only for *you*; an extraordinary life is one that is lived for *others*. Our lives and our leadership are measured by our impact and influence on those around us.

The bottom line is this:

In a world that seems to be coming unglued faster than ever before—the racial and economic divides continue to grow, religious intolerance has reached record levels, and war is becoming the normal way of life rather than some isolated event—it is going to take *extraordinary* efforts by *extraordinary* people to become the glue that puts this world back together again.

So do you want to be ordinary or extraordinary?

I believe YOU are extraordinary!

The Most Influential Person in Your Life

Martin Luther King, Jr. once spoke of the influence that Jackie Robinson had on his life: "You will never know what you [Don Newcombe] and Jackie and Roy [Campanella] did to make it possible to do my job."

All three of the men that King mentioned were baseball players! They weren't politicians or CEOs; they were athletes. Those men were amazing and talented players who used their passion and talent for the game of baseball to impact one of the most influential men in the history of our world.

So, the next time you think your WHY or your talents aren't good enough because they aren't (blank) enough, think again. Anything you do in this world has the power to impact and change the world; the only thing stopping you from doing that is *you*.

You are the one telling yourself it isn't good enough...which is why the only opinion that really matters is your own.

People may say that you couldn't ever use sports or art or being a veterinarian to really impact the world, but it only matters if **you believe that**. If you know you can use that to leave this world better than you found it, then you will.

YOU choose your influence. Not anyone else.

YOU choose how you'll leave your mark on the world. Society doesn't choose that for you.

YOU choose your impact. No one else can do that for you.

Making the choice to believe YOU can make a difference is the simplest thing you can do, and simultaneously, it is the hardest thing to carry out every day. So on the days when it's hard, things don't make sense, or someone is trying to ensure you don't move forward, obsess over your WHY so much that you keep moving forward.

Your ability to create true change comes from your ability to inspire people to action, not from your ability to look out for number one and ensure your level of comfort on this earth remains undisturbed.

Now, don't freak out. This doesn't mean you have to be this super charismatic, outgoing, great speaker, or that you have to inspire millions of people around the world.

> "We have the power to define ourselves: by telling our own stories, in our own words, with our own voices."
>
> —*Sarah Kay*

All this means is you need to have a strong WHY that you completely obsess over, and then communicate that to people.

So what does that look like for someone who is not a public speaker or does not have a traditional leadership platform? Here are two examples:

- Let's say your purpose is to help people live more fulfilled lives, and your mission is to enable people to live longer and healthier lives through advances in science. So your WHY—the thing that compels you forward—is using your brainpower to make new scientific discoveries.

- Now let's say you were bullied in school. Can you stop all the bullies from being cruel to other kids? Not directly, no. But if you discover that your purpose in life is to help kids make other kids feel loved, and your mission is to eradicate bullying, then you can start pursuing your WHY by having a conversation with the five people that sit at your lunch table every day, your leader at youth group, and your sports team...

The point isn't how well you do it or how many people hear it. All you have to do is **start**! Start with those closest to you and let them hear about what moves you.

When you begin to inspire people with your WHY, they will follow you in your journey because their motivation to follow comes from within. They have deeply resonated with your WHY and that means more than bribes or great prizes to be gained if they join a cause or following.

Their heart is in their actions, and that motivation will keep people following your WHY until the end.

> "Every achiever I have ever met says, "My life turned around when I began to believe in me."
>
> —*Robert Schuller*

You don't need to *convince* people to follow; just start conversations. Tell them about your WHY and if it resonates, you'll have them on board for life.

People don't care about *what* or *how*... they care about WHY.

Your WHY is simply the most effective, inspiring and motivating line you can utter, and just doing that will inspire people, because it's exactly the opposite of how everyone else is communicating to those same people.

So what is everyone else communicating?

It seems to me that everyone is trying to _pitch_ something—the latest idea, the latest trend, the latest... anything. We have become so used to getting pitched that we are ready to say no the moment someone opens his or her mouth.

So don't sell...just have a conversation.

Because one conversation can change the whole world.

Let There Be Light!

Just when you thought it was impossible for any more elephants to fit in the room, the third and final one has finally shown itself.

We've already confronted and thrown *perfection* out the door. We looked at *failure* and saw that it is our friend and not our enemy. And now comes a four-letter word that no one likes to utter:

FEAR.

We are not going to completely eradicate fear. What we are going to do instead is turn the light on in the room and expose the fear for what it really is—a good thing.

You just thought you read this wrong.

I used to agree with you, but not anymore.

Here's the deal...

Fear is actually your body's gift to you. The fear you feel before a big test, speech, game or before doing something new, is your body giving you exactly what you need to complete the task ahead of you.

We've been taught and conditioned to call that feeling within us *fear*, and when that fear comes, we should run; it's the simple notion known as "fight or flight."

Instead, we should be **thanking** our bodies and using it to help us complete the task before us.

It's completely normal to be terrified, even scared out of your mind, before you are about to do something big, meaningful and brave. And every single time you are about to step into something that is going to change the game, you will probably feel afraid.

In fact, just by reading this book, you are challenging yourself to embark on a journey of impact and change—and that's scary, but it's also great.

Consequently, fear comes about as a result of how we think. If we let fear be fear, we won't want to take action.

If we see fear as a gift and as a tool designed to be used to push on and succeed, nothing can stop us.

The media, friends, strangers, and others have been telling us for years to fear, to play small, and to dream small. We've been told to be afraid because we aren't good enough, smart enough, and we'll never make it as an artist, singer, teacher, astronaut, or tech CEO.

We've been told that since "no one in your family ever did anything great or had any success, how could you?"

Why bother, right? Your fate is sealed because of how you look, where you're from, and the grades you got in school.

RIGHT??

WRONG!!

Turn the light on these lies and let fear say what it needs to say. Then you can reply with a "thanks but no thanks!" and use those feelings to motivate you to keep dreaming and keep BEing the change.

Consider fear to be a friendly reminder that you are the glue—and the world <u>needs</u> you to keep moving forward.

Graduation is Just the Beginning

Servant leadership is about serving the people within your WHY and helping them get to where ***they*** need to go. When you walk down the path of your WHY, people will begin to follow— and *that* is when you have the opportunity to help them get to where they dream to go because of their own WHY.

These are the people that belong in what I like to call your ***Area of Influence***. Seth Godin calls these people your "tribe." They are the individuals you are both directly *and* indirectly influencing every day, even when you think people aren't watching.

You have a purpose and a mission, and no matter where you are in your journey, you have people watching and looking up to you. You have people waiting for you to be brave, to show up, and to lead them.

What you do with that substantial influence is up to you— and if you decide you want to make the most of your influence and use your WHY to help others, what's the next step?

First, you need to have more of those "I believe" conversations. In fact, that is probably one of the most important activities you will ever engage in on a daily basis. But even more fundamentally than that, there is something else you need to be doing every day and every week to keep growing and becoming a better leader.

It's one of the most important and yet most *overlooked* action items for the younger generation—and that is learning.

I'm not talking about the kind of "learning" we do at school. That is just the beginning. After we graduate high school and college, we've just barely scratched the surface of learning.

> "There is no end to education. It is not that you read a book, pass an examination, and finish with education. The whole of life, from the moment you are born to the moment you die, is a process of learning."
> —*Jiddu Krishnamurti*

For this reason, I want to dispel the myth right now that learning is reserved just for your school years. So many young people dream of the day they'll graduate and never have to go to school again, but learning can't and shouldn't stop at graduation.

When I was in high school, my dad would often go to business conferences and trainings. These three- to four-day conferences went for ten hours a day and featured various speakers and trainers. He would come home exhausted, and I always thought it was because he was old (no offense, dad).

He would also regularly use his driving and flying time to read books and listen to CDs about business and personal growth—and I thought, "Eww, that sounds so boring."

I couldn't *wait* to get out of school, but he always told me that I should <u>never</u> stop being in school. Of course, back then, I didn't believe him or take him seriously, and I certainly never thought I'd be saying the same thing to you! At 17, I finally had the chance to go to a conference with him, and I couldn't believe how much I learned—and how tired I was! It was exhausting but so worthwhile, and I've been soaking up every chance I get to learn something new. As leaders, we need to be constantly learning and growing; it will make us better leaders and better human beings.

One friend actually texted me to ask me whether my dad forced me to go, or I genuinely wanted to go to that conference. Like so many of us, she believed that learning is reserved only for school, so why would anyone in their right minds willingly subject themselves to more teaching??

This is small thinking, and it is the kind of mindset that will significantly block the reach of your influence.

During school and beyond, you have access to an entire world full of knowledge, experience and wisdom. Don't spend your time at school on your phone or chatting with your friends; sit up and pay attention. Even when you don't like the subject or find the lecture boring, find one thing you take away from the class. Then go home and look up a part of the lesson that interested you.

You are an example in your school, and people will

> "Live as if you were to die tomorrow. Learn as if you were to live forever."
>
> **—Mahatma Gandhi**

notice if you choose to soak up every word and respect your teachers. Step up and lead with an appetite for learning and a deep respect for those who are willing to teach you.

Always remember that leadership is a balance of both theory and practice. You need to continue doing and BEing—but you also need to grow. And the only way to do that is to remain a sponge. Soak up wisdom; soak up the actions of the pioneers who have been where you want to go.

Have you ever heard the saying, "The speed of the leader is the speed of the team?"

It's a powerful statement and oh so true.

If you've ever had a coach or leader who is truly inspiring and motivating—one of those few people in life who made a lasting impression on you—I bet you can just *think* about that coach or leader and feel inspired to go take action.

When you, as a leader, are growing and reaching new heights, those within your Area of Influence will be on fire as well. But if you slow down and go into "coasting" mode and stop learning, the momentum and the inspiration you radiate will also fade.

Don't be the kind of leader who makes the mistake of thinking that once they get a few people believing in them and their WHY, that they can sit back and let the process run on auto pilot.

It simply doesn't work that way.

It's you—*you* are the catalyst of change—and you are the glue that holds the process together. Don't take this role lightly; keep your momentum by embracing learning for the rest of your life.

Never stop learning!

"People who make the choice to study, work hard or do whatever they endeavor is to give it the max on themselves to reach to the top level. And you have the people who get envy and jealous, yet are not willing to put that work in, and they want to get the same praise."

—Evander Holyfield

"Almost nothing matters about your circumstances except your mindset; situations will always change so the only way to overcome and to win is with the right mindset."

—*Anni Keffer*

8

Start Now!

YOU'VE REACHED THE end! How does it feel?

Of course, it may be the end of this book, but it's only the beginning of your new leadership journey.

Too often, at the end of any book—even the ones we love—we close its pages and set it aside. It goes on the shelf and a few weeks later, it's like we never read it. It simply becomes a two-inch wide space holder on a dusty bookshelf filled with good intentions.

And so you've reached yet another choice:

- OPTION 1: You can allow what you learned in this book to be pushed aside for another, more convenient day, because you're too busy to start changing things right now. Next year will be the year, right?

OR...

- OPTION 2: You can decide to BE the change you have desperately wished to see in your world and start now.

I don't know about you, but I've got enough books on my bookshelf. Instead of shelving this book, may I suggest that you keep it out and use it as a field guide as you embark on this exciting time in your life?

Because guess what? You ARE old enough. You ARE smart enough. You ARE enough today, right now, to change the world.

Use the lessons in this book and the clarity I hope it brought you to propel you into making the changes to become a better leader and leave a lasting and powerful legacy behind you.

For now, let's use our last few pages together to start the process of dreaming big, proclaiming your obsessed-over WHY, and changing your world.

Such an important journey can't be traveled in a lukewarm manner. Being a lukewarm leader means you have one foot in the servant leadership world and the other foot out the door and back inside the Matrix.

Living with one foot in and one foot out is a torturous way to live your life. When you find yourself unable or unwilling to fully commit to pursuing your WHY with everything you have, you'll use your circumstances and the lies we've been led to believe (you're too young, you're not [blank] enough, etc.) as excuses to live a half-baked, watered-down existence.

The kind of leadership we discussed in this book calls for your heart to be all in, with both feet planted and ready to stay the course despite the ups and downs and the obstacles.

If you have decided you want to be a *leader on fire*, then congratulations! I want to leave you with an acronym that will help you remember three important things as you continue on this journey.

One of these things you must seek out, and the other two require you to put up your dukes and fight! The three things start with your M.O.M… because mothers usually know best, right?

Mindset
Others
Models

We'll quickly talk about each one of these important reminders as our time together (for now anyway) draws to a close.

<u>M</u> = Mindset

Mindset is a simple word that carries so much weight. It's an extremely vital piece of the puzzle that will make or break your pursuit of servant leadership. When it comes to getting your mind right and in the game, you have to instill 24/7 monitoring and total control over <u>the</u> most vulnerable areas for anyone and everyone—and that is our minds.

Personally, my mindset has been the biggest obstacle in my life. Over the years, I have belittled myself, believed lies and played small. I used to consistently stop myself from reaching higher and doing more because of what was going on not *around* me, but *inside* me.

I am not one to become steeped in regret, but it's tempting to look back on my high school and college years and feel remorseful about how many opportunities I missed because of the lies I programmed my mind to believe.

Instead, I choose to not dwell on past mistakes and view those years as a necessary part of my journey. I learned so much from all of those self-inflicted disappointments, and now I am better able to equip you with tools that will enable you to bypass a lot of the struggles I faced.

You might be thinking, "But Anni, aren't we just talking about our thoughts here? Could those really be so powerful?"

Oh, they are. In fact, *everything* you do in life (and don't do) starts with your mind.

Think about it: Have you ever been working out and feel completely exhausted, but you know you have one more exercise left or one mile left on your run? Your body is screaming, "Stop!" but you choose to keep going. You choose to tell yourself that you can do it; you can push just one final time.

What happens in those moments? You reprogram what your body is telling your mind—which is to stop immediately—and your mind orders your body to keep going.

We talked earlier about how your brain is like a computer, with the ability to be programmed to believe whatever you tell it to believe. In the example above, in the final moments of a tough workout, you can actually program your mind to believe that you can keep going even though your body doesn't feel like it can!

Even though you feel like you have nothing left, your brain can provide your body with enough fuel to push through the exhaustion and complete your workout.

Now *that* is powerful!

Unfortunately, that power works both ways. We are constantly programming our minds to believe negative lies and message—and if we think those untruths enough, our brains will be programmed to believe every word. Your mind is your body's control station, and your body is at your mind's mercy. In short:

Your head is the one calling all the shots.

More often than not, it's not that others stop us dead in our tracks—it's our own minds! That is why every day you spend beating yourself up and engaging in negative self-

talk, the harder it will be to break your mind of what you have long programmed it to believe and do. Not to mention you delay opportunities that may arise for you to step up and lead with your WHY.

You can be your own greatest and deadliest enemy—and *you* are your biggest obstacle in your leadership journey. It's like you are driving along in your car, and suddenly you screech to a halt, jump out and roll a gigantic stone onto the road, completely blocking your path.

You wouldn't do that, would you? Then why do you put up roadblocks in your mind?

What's really interesting is we could name so many other kinds of roadblocks we face in our journeys (critics, lack of talent or education, our past, etc.) but we never seem to call out the main culprit—our own selves. None of those other "roadblocks" will even matter unless we *let* them matter—and that starts with what you program your mind to believe and do.

Throughout this book I have talked about choices, and that is because this life is all about your choices, and here's where the rubber meets the road:

Are you going to be the kind of person who chooses to see immovable rocks blocking every path, or will you fight and press on past the obstacles?

When the stuff hits the fan, everything is going wrong, people are pulling you down and you can't seem to think anything positive about your abilities or influence, what do you do? How do you overcome the urge to give up and give in?

Here is an exercise that has greatly helped me in my battle with keeping my mindset right, and I recommend you try it the next time you have any kind of negative thought about your gifts, your talents, or your purpose:

Mindset Drill

1. When you feel a negative thought clawing its way into the forefront of your mind, grab a piece of paper or a note card and a pen.

2. Write down each individual negative thought on its own piece of paper.

3. Stick those pieces of paper in a small bag and put the bag away for an hour. Go do other things, and after an hour, come back to the bag.

4. Dump out all of the thoughts, lies and negative messages and read each card out loud.

5. After you read each lie your brain tried to make you believe, state the real truth. Here is how that might look:

Negative Thought:
"I have nothing to offer the world."

You *know* that's not true, but your mind is powerful and has the ability to turn ridiculous lies into realities. So, after you've spoken it aloud, dispute that lie with something positive you have done recently. Maybe you helped a friend through a tough time, cleaned up for your parents without them having to ask, did great on a speech in your class, or got a compliment at work.

The positive thing doesn't have to be some world changing accomplishment; you are simply recognizing everyday actions that were positive and helped someone along the way.

This exercise is not going to be easy at first, especially if this is an area where you really struggle. All you need to do, though, is try! Anything worth doing takes time and practice.

This drill will help you put the lies, problems and doubts into perspective by comparing them to reality. That is the whole point—to get them out of your head and compare it to the real truth.

I recently conducted a similar exercise with a group of girls to whom I was speaking. We were discussing the power of our self-talk and how damaging it can be. I had each of the girls write down on a sticky note a lie about themselves that they believe. I collected the notes and stuck all of them on one of the girls, and then I proceeded to read each of the lies out loud.

They included things like:

- I'm ugly.

- I have no purpose.

- I'm deformed.

- Too fat.

- I'll never be loved.

- Too stupid.

After reading the notecards, it was hard not to burst into tears. We all felt the sadness of hearing those lies read aloud. After I had finished saying them all, the room was so silent you could hear a pin drop.

The spoken words stung far worse than the girls could have ever imagined. Why? Because lies always sound so much better in your head. When you choose to say them out loud, you *hear* the pain they cause.

Words have destroyed countries and races throughout our history. Words have started wars, ended relationships, and caused irreparable damage.

What do you think they're doing to you?

After we read the lies, I asked them to take another note card and write down a truth about them in order to replace the lies with the true, beautiful reality. These truths included statements such as:

- I have a purpose.

- I'm chosen.

- I'm intentionally created.

- I was made for a reason.

- I'm deeply loved.

After we read these out loud, everything in the room changed. It was like someone opened up a window and a fresh breeze came rushing in. There was a sense of purpose, and we could all breathe and feel warmth.

Words have power, both in your head and spoken aloud.

Sure, "sticks and stones may break our bones," but bones mend. Words, on the other hand, can destroy—and heal—us like nothing else.

Somewhere along the way we stopped believing we were made for something bigger than just existing. At some point we stopped being able to look in the mirror and say, "You look gooooood. Now go kick some butt."

What happened? Who told you that you aren't beautiful, chosen and intentionally made?

To whoever helped you to believe differently, say "I'm on to you and your lies, and I won't believe you anymore!"

And then go stand up for the truth—in your own life and in the lives of those in your Area of Influence.

O = Others

From the day we are born, society places us into neat little white boxes. They have pretty labels, fancy wrapping and tight seals. These boxes allow others to easily understand us and put us in our exact right place in society. Here are a few of those boxes:

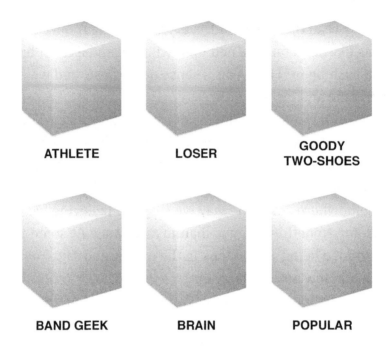

ATHLETE   LOSER   GOODY TWO-SHOES

BAND GEEK   BRAIN   POPULAR

These labels help those around us know how to interact with us—whether to shun us, ignore us, mock us, or want to be our friends.

Most people don't know how to break free of the boxes in which society places us, so here's the big secret:

The power comes in recognizing the box in the first place, and once you realize that you've been placed inside a box, it's time to bust out!

You CAN learn what it feels like to live a life without labels, but first, you have to choose to either live within the confines in which others placed you or live according to your *own* rules, governed by your WHY.

By breaking out of your own box, you are giving people permission to do the same. Once you break free, you will have the unique opportunity to help others break out of their boxes and learn that they too can do something extraordinary.

People often don't know what to do with people like us—the dreamers, doers and leaders—because we don't follow the same plan, rules and regulations.

That's fine by me! I don't want to be predictable. I don't want to be ordinary or basic.

Be the courageous one. Show other people how to be themselves. Show other people how to change the world around them.

People are waiting for you to walk the path before they'll walk behind you.

M = Models

And now it's time for an important announcement: ***You can't lead without role models in your life. You really can't.***
You can *try*, and you may be able to enjoy some success for short periods of time. But role models are necessary if you want to be a world changer.

Those who have been where you want to be—those who are older or more experienced—can provide you with a roadmap that will help you set your sights more clearly on your destination and the path you need to take in order to get there.

Role models can also help you navigate through situations and experiences and consistently challenge you to be a better leader.

In the quest for the right role models for your life, look for those that have lived their WHY and are ***still*** living it out.

People who once had a purpose and a well-defined mission but are no longer pursuing it are not good examples. Acting as a leader and following your WHY should be two actions that you execute until the day you die.

A role model could be someone you've *never even met*—and those types of leaders can be excellent examples to emulate.

However, you should also be looking for those you *can meet* with on a somewhat regular basis. Such role models are also called "mentors." Mentors can be coaches, teachers, or leaders in your youth group. They are people whose actions you can observe to see if they are ones you want to model your own after.

There is almost no end to the types of role models that may be right for you and the pursuit of your WHY. But in case you are new to the idea of having role models, it's best to follow the Role Model "Rule of 3." You should always have these three people in your life:

1. **Elder Role Model**. Someone older and/or more successful than you that you can learn from, ask questions and duplicate their actions.

2. **Peer Role Model**. A peer on your level with whom you can "do" life and work through situations and seasons together.

3. **Role Model in Training**. Someone that you mentor on a regular basis. This keeps you accountable and fosters your continual growth (as well as the growth of your mentee).

We have talked several times about your **Area of Influence**— those you both directly and indirectly affect with your words and actions—and now we need to bring up one other group.

This is your **Circle of Influence**—those who you let influence you and the people with whom you surround yourself. These would include your role models and mentors as well as friends, peers and others you come into contact with on a regular basis.

The two circles can contain some of the same people, but they have two different purposes.

AREA OF INFLUENCE

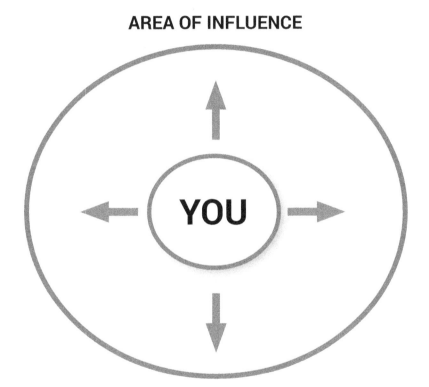

Your WHY flows OUT to others.

Your **Area of Influence** is the people around you who are influenced by what you put out into the space around you. *You* control the flow of information—it goes **OUT** from you, the source, when you start conversations that include your "I believe" statements and talking about your WHY with everyone and anyone who will listen.

CIRCLE OF INFLUENCE

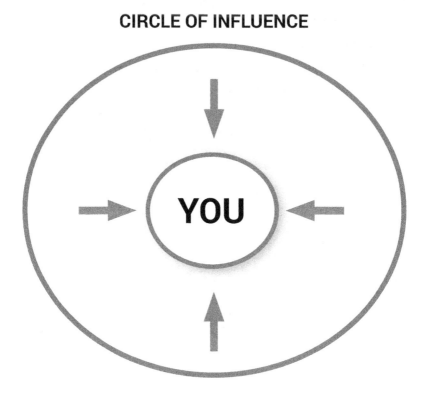

You choose what influences flow IN to you.

Your **Circle of Influence**, on the other hand, is comprised of those you **allow** in to be a part of your life. You still have control, but this time the information (aka the influence others have on your life) flows IN to you. This is *your* circle and you must be extremely protective of who has access to it.

This circle has nothing to do with fitting in, being in the popular crowd, or being one of the cool kids. It has everything to do with the understanding of the impact those closest to you have on your life.

Those in nearest proximity to you have the unique ability to completely change the direction you are going in, for good or for bad.

As Jim Rohn once said, "***You're the average of the five people you spend the most time with.***"

This also means that:

- You make the average amount of money of the 5 people you spend the most time with.

- You give the average amount of money of the 5 people **you spend the most time with.**

- Your actions will be the average of the 5 people you spend the most time with.

- Your beliefs will be the average of the 5 people you spend the most time with.

So yeah, the people in your circle of influence matter—a lot.

This doesn't mean tomorrow you should stop being friends with everyone. Not the point. But take time to reflect on which of your friends are building you up and pushing you to be a better person and leader.

Say you're standing on a chair and you're trying to get your friend up on the chair to join you. You keep trying to pull your friend up, but it's super difficult and takes forever to get him up on the chair, if you do at all.

Now imagine that your friend is trying to pull you off of the chair onto the ground where he is—it's incredibly easy.

The point is it's so much easier for your friends to negatively influence you than it is for you to positively influence them.

This shouldn't stop you from trying to influence them; it should instead be a warning to remind you of how easily we are influenced by our friends.

Your circle of influence will largely determine whether you will be ordinary or extraordinary. Allow me to illustrate:

There once was a man who was tired of living an average life. He wanted to do something more, so he asked a wealthy man for the secret to his success. After listing hard work as a primary reason, the rich man told the ordinary man that his real secret was "to keep the right company."

The ordinary man listened to the advice, and he decided to make a clean sweep in his life and remove all of the negative people, the naysayers, and the dream killers from his network. So he made a simple list—it had a column for people who would improve his life, and a column for people who would drag him down.

For those who could improve his life, he spent as much time around them as possible. If someone might drag him down, he never spent more than five minutes around that person.

After adhering strictly to his list for just three years, the man finally fulfilled his dream of becoming a millionaire.[2]

You may think it's not possible to cut some people out of your life (even if you know they are not good influences on you), and that's okay. The point here is this: Spend as much time around people who are leading well and living out their WHY in big ways.

Ask questions, meet with those positive influences regularly, and study their habits. Their influence alone will make a massive difference in your life.

---

[2] http://addicted2success.com/success-advice/why-successful-people-leave-their-loser-friends-be-hind/?utm_source=crowdignite.com&utm_medium=referral&utm_campaign=crowdignite.com

You need those kinds of people in your life—and they need you! People are desperately searching for someone to follow. They're looking for someone or something to stand behind. And yes, it can and should be you!

Answer the Calling

Whether on a local or a global scale, the desperate need for leaders is there. This world needs leaders who are kind and humble, gracious and bold, and hungry to leave an impact.

Will you step up and answer the call?

If you answered yes, then let's get real... What are you going to do NOW? It's great to learn about leadership, but what matters is what you do with it. So answer these questions to help you take that first step:

1. What change do you want to see in the world?

_____

_____

_____

2. Who do you know who also wants to see that change happen in the world?

_____

_____

_____

3. Who else could you tell about this change you want to see?

_____

_____

_____

4. How are you going to make this change happen?

_____

_____

_____

Once you answer these questions I want you to copy these answers onto a separate sheet of paper or rip this page out right out of this book (you're a pro at that now anyway!).

Next, I want you to tape these answers where you will see them each day (your bathroom mirror, in your car, somewhere in your room). In fact, tape these right next to your WHY. The more places you display your inspirations, the more likely you are to start moving towards the direction of change.

When you hear or see a goal every day, then guess what? Yep, you are **training your brain** to find ways to achieve that goal.

The way you bring about change in this world will probably be different than the way others do, and that's not a bad thing—that's actually a great thing!

Each of us, with our unique talents and gifts, view the problems we are most passionate about fixing in different ways. And sometimes the solutions to those problems are presented to us in ways we never imagined.

For example:

- Rosa Parks used public demonstration on a bus.
- Helen Keller used storytelling despite her physical disabilities.
- Oprah used influence through a TV show.
- Blake Mycoskie used shoes.

It doesn't matter what methods or paths you use; it just matters that you do something.

So what will you use to change the world?

All you need is YOU and your WHY.

So go out, dear friend, and leave this world brighter, more alive and filled with servant leaders like you who are passionately obsessed with their WHY and with leaving a legacy here on Earth.

> ## "You were not born a winner, and you were not born a loser. You are what you make yourself be."
> ### *—Lou Holtz*

Special Message:

Live Your Why!

Start Now!

About Anni

ANNI KEFFER IS a nationally-recognized Author, Youth Leadership Speaker, Entrepreneur and Founder of the Young Women of Influence Conference.

She has been seen in CBS, ABC, NBC, FOX affiliates and in a number of publications, including the *New York Business Journal, Pittsburgh Post-Gazette, Miami Herald, Chicago Business Journal, WHIRL, San Francisco Chronicle, MompreneurMedia* and others.

She is the Author of *Leadership Built On Why* and a Co-Author of *Girls Lead.*

Anni was nominated for *WHIRL Magazine's* Women In Business 2016. Anni loves to read, teach, take adventures and she calls Pittsburgh, Pennsylvania her home.

THE IDEAL PROFESSIONAL SPEAKER FOR YOUR NEXT EVENT!

Any organization that wants to develop their people to become "extraordinary," needs to hire Anni for a keynote and/or workshop training!

TO CONTACT OR BOOK ANNI TO SPEAK:

2535 Washington Rd. Suite 1120
Pittsburgh, PA 15241

1-800-853-6250

www.AnniKeffer.com

MOTIVATE AND INSPIRE OTHERS!

"Share This Book"

Retail $24.95

Special Quantity Discounts

5-20 Books	$16.95
21-99 Books	$13.95
100-499 Books	$10.95
500-999 Books	$6.95
1,000+ Books	$4.95

To Place an Order Contact:

2535 Washington Rd. Suite 1120
Pittsburgh, PA 15241
1-800-853-6250
www.AnniKeffer.com

Made in the USA
Monee, IL
16 November 2019